THE HUMAN FIRM

JOIN THE HUMAN REVOLUTION,
GO BEYOND DIGITAL
AND BUILD A SCALABLE,
CLIENT-CENTRIC FIRM

WILL FARNELL

Contents

Foreword 5

Introduction 11

MAKING A START 15
The Future is Bright, The Future is Human 17
The Engagement Correlation 29
Difference is Beautiful 41
Generation Shift and Buying Behaviours 51
The Living Brand 59
Business, Marketing and the Mindset of Nice 71

MAKING IT GROW 87
Scalability, Staff and Super-Evolution 89
Scalability and the De-Willing Progression 97
Staff and Scalability 107
Scalability and the Human Firm 117

MAKING A DIFFERENCE 121
In the Numbers 123
Purpose, the Underlying Driver 131
Client Lifetime Value 141

MAKING IT HUMAN 149
Making it Human 151
Culture, Personality and Experience 157
The Point of Touchpoints 171
Know your Client for Genuine Insight 177
Insights and Advisory 187

MAKING IT WORK **195**
Digital to Human, Why a Click of a Switch isn't Enough **197**
Consider your Processes **207**

MAKING IT OUT **215**
Tribalism and the New Landscape of Sharing **217**
Too Much Noise **221**

MAKING IT COHERENT **231**
Agile Visions: from Lifetime Value to Future Proofing **233**
In Conclusion **243**

APPENDICES **247**
We Want Your Feedback **249**
Why I Chose Sage **250**
Sage **253**
Acknowledgements **254**
About the Contributors **257**
Conversations **265**
Glossary **280**

Will Farnell and James Ashford on a GoProposal business trip in San Jose.

Foreword

James Ashford, Founder of GoProposal by Sage

Technology has elevated you into a position where you can forge deep, meaningful, long lasting, impactful relationships with other humans (your clients), who in turn, care deeply about the work they do and the humans they interact with. If you stop and think about the number of lives you touch, it's huge. Just think about the number of clients you have and their partners and children, the number of staff they have and their families, the number of suppliers who serve them and the number of clients they serve. Through the work you do, you touch all those people's lives in some way

Creating a Human Firm is about being aware of those human connections. Through these genuine interactions you can grow and contribute and this is where you find the highest levels of fulfilment. This is why you entered this profession in the first place. Accounting will always be a heart-centred profession filled with tough conversations, tears, hard work and moments of celebration. You get the great privilege of intimate access into the finances, hopes, dreams and fears of your client's businesses and the personal lives on which they build their successes, but only if you show up as humans yourself.

Compliance distracted you from this for many years. Advisory has lit the fire again. Digitisation gave you hope but then served as a distraction in its own right. You thought it was the end goal, but it was not. It was the gateway. And as your firm evolves through this digital gateway, you can return to your roots and your calling. You can uncouple yourself from who you were told you needed to be. You can unshackle yourself from the fears you imposed on yourself. Finally you can connect with a world full of excitement in the realm of the human.

Theologian and humanitarian Albert Schweitzer wrote *"The purpose of human life is to serve, and to show compassion and the will to help others."* You could conclude this is the purpose of The Human Firm – to serve clients, to show them compassion, and to assist.

Throughout this book, Will Farnell generously shares the journey his own firm has travelled, from becoming and being a fully Digital Firm, to being a Human Firm, and the journey he has helped many other firms through, with his coaching. Farnell Clarke was the first full cloud-based accounting firm in the world, the first through the digital gateway, and has led many other pioneering initiatives ever since. The learnings Will shares here have been hard won, and pressure tested. Not everything has worked perfectly, which Will is quick to share so that you can avoid some of the collisions his pioneering endeavours inevitably encountered. Collisions that are always the case with the first through the wall.

In his first book, he showed how to create The Digital Firm, which created the gateway through that wall. In this book, he paves the way for you to evolve beyond that, to become a Human Firm. This isn't fluffy theory. This is not the soft stuff. This is hard, and comes with a sense of great urgency. The Human Firm isn't optional, it's inevitable, because if you act like robots, you will be replaced by them. The only protection against this is to build a human firm, now and with haste.

You will find this book challenging in parts, illuminating throughout and very actionable. And if you take those actions, maybe you will unlock tremendous value for your clients, your team and yourself.

I have been in the accounting industry for the best part of a decade, helping accountants and bookkeepers to price their services more profitably, sell them more confidently and deliver the greatest impact they possibly can to their clients. My passion to succeed in this mission is because first and foremost, I'm a client of these accounting and bookkeeping services myself.

I've run a business where I knew what I wanted, but not what I needed. That led to massively underinvesting in the finance function of that company, which failed. I've also received tremendous value and benefit from accounting and bookkeeping services, which led to the successful scaling and exit of a business. By the time I came to sell that business, I was investing upwards of £5,000 a month into its finance function through the accounting firm we were working with. When I first started working with them, I spent £750 a month. That was still three times what I was spending with my previous accountant. The reason I was prepared to make that higher investment, wasn't because I understood their services better, it was because I felt they understood me better.

They knew what our family's long-term financial goals were, and how much we'd need to sell the business for to achieve them. They knew that my immediate goals were to take my children to school every day, move closer to their school and to get my wife out of full-time employment.

On the first page of every set of monthly management accounts, I was reminded of those goals. The meeting would always start with... "How many times have you taken your kids to school this week?" "Have you put an offer in on a house yet?" "Has Bekki handed in her notice yet?" "What does the business need to do to achieve those goals?" "How can we help your business do that?"

One year, I remember working with them to set the budget and forecast for the year and they asked how many customers we wanted to get to. I said *"1,000." "1,000?"* They challenged; *"Why?"*

"Well it's 1,000 isn't it?" My ego said. *"But it doesn't mean anything,"* they replied. *"What do you want to achieve as a family this year? What would make life better?" What would be a great year for you?"*

So we thought, and planned, and concluded that it would be for me personally to earn £10,000 a month after tax, and to go to Lapland with the kids that year. We agreed that would be a great year.

And that's what happened, because we were intentional in setting business goals that primarily facilitated the life we wanted. Accounting isn't about spreadsheets, P&L accounts, bookkeeping or tech. Done properly, it's about enabling your clients to live the lives they want. That only happens when you stop putting your services or the tech at the centre of what you do, and start putting your client there instead. Not your client as a "business", but your client as a person, as a human, with fears and dreams and hopes and rough edges. You see, your commercial value in the world is directly proportional to the size of the problems you can solve.

Completing my bookkeeping is a relatively low value problem to solve, but if doing so enables me to take my kids to school every day and to focus on my highest and best activities at work, then it solves a far higher value problem.

Producing a budget and a forecast are relatively low value problems to solve, but if doing so helps me to achieve the business goals that enables me to take my family to Lapland and meet Santa that same year, they solve a far higher value problem.

However, you would only know that if you were to have very human conversations with the clients you serve. You would only know that if you connect the value of what you do to the problems and opportunities that show up in your client's lives.

That, in essence, is what a human firm is all about.

James Ashford and family visiting Santa in Lapland.

Farnell
+
Clarke
=
ccountancy

Introduction

Five years after **The Digital Firm** I am here to share the next paradigm shift in our profession.

It is a shift in attitude from relatively impersonal compliance-based processes towards a deepening of authentic human relationships, full circle back to the way accounting started. Based on regular communications and the associated provision of value–added insights to the client, it sounds simple but isn't. It results in deep change, an increase in competitiveness and a level of future proofing that is vital for the accountancy firm's survival.

The writing is on the wall. Despite Covid driving firms to work more in the cloud, despite Making Tax Digital (MTD) for small businesses, and despite an increase in automated service provision by new tech providers, most firms still make their money from compliance. Even now, few firms are fully digital (and by that I mean entirely cloud-based and supported by appropriate end-to-end processes).

Faced with these important challenges in compliance practice and accounting services over the coming decade – including digital compliance requirements, AI and clients with an increasingly cloud-based digital approach to information processing – firms have to change to survive. My accountancy firm Farnell Clarke is thinking and working towards the next evolution of the human firm as the only logical step to stay at the leading edge of a constantly evolving and increasingly competitive environment.

In The Digital Firm I wrote "the accounting market landscape will be unrecognisable in another five years' time," and that doing nothing, while a choice, would result in firms going out of business. I got the timing wrong, clearly. But the market is changing. Firms can continue to bury their heads in the sand and do nothing, knowing that eventually clients will leave for organisations able to provide added value services or simply to take advantage of a reduced cost of compliance.

That so few firms have made the shift – even now – is an advantage for early adopters. As for Farnell Clarke? The implementation of our vision continues. No longer the flighty teenager, we are still doing things somewhat differently. Hopefully this book, which summarises what we've learned during our leading-and-occasionally-bleeding-edge evolution, will help you accelerate your shift to a Human Firm, and maximise the benefits of doing so.

Like my previous book, The Human Firm is primarily based on my experience; if the text is unattributed, assume it's me. I've joined with Sage to produce it, and because I want to give you the best possible choices, I've brought in experts and independent case studies to give a more balanced perspective. By doing so, I aim to provide senior managers with a quick overview, more details should they be interested, and the confidence that what follows is worth passing on to staff.

Book Structure

The book is in seven sections, (eight if you count the appendices, but who does!) Making a Start is about setting the scene, Making it Grow about scaling your firm, Making a Difference is about how to differentiate the firm and how you might measure progress, Making it Human is the nub of the book, (although the Human theme runs throughout the whole book), Making it Work covers practical aspects, Making it Out is about context and choices and Making it Coherent is about sustainability, future proofing and – of course – exit strategy.

Before each section is a tiny preview, and before each chapter a quote that shows the tone of the following chapter. After that comes the body of the chapter and there are take-away notes at the end.

Farnell Clarke has made the mistakes so that you don't have to. That's what the 'Will to Learn' sections are about. They share important learning points and a few epiphanies.

I've started each chapter with quotes; something I said five-years ago, and what I'm saying now. It's a shorthand to show how Farnell Clarke's approach has changed, if indeed it has. You'll also find quotes in each chapter from conversations I've had with interesting people covering things as diverse as case studies, opinions and future predictions. They're very revealing, and give different perspectives and takes on what I discuss in the book. You can find more of these non-Will perspectives in the appendix and the conversations themselves are available online.

Notes

PART ONE

MAKING A START

Tech, Tech, Tech. Digital, Digital, Digital.

The Human side of accounting, while lost in translation has never been more important. It's time to turn the record over and start thinking about what that tech enables us to do.

This section sets the scene, examines the context and takes a longer term view. It considers what matters in terms of communication and looks at how we might think of the quality and duration of that communication. It talks about good habits, a firm's obligation, the changing needs and expectations of different generations, about the difference between branding and personality, the need to change our mindsets, and how all of the above should be considered when you're working on differentiating your firm.

Through digital and back,
to close the client centric circle

1

The Future is Bright, The Future is Human

THEN

"The new digital practice utilises a mix of digital technology and digitally aware staff to deliver first-class services effectively and efficiently through maximum levels of automation."

NOW

"To become a fully Human Firm, you first need to be fully digital."

As I write this book, we are faced with a major cost of living crisis and huge uncertainty around the economy. I believe that the challenges we will face over the next 12 to 24 months are far greater than those we faced during the global pandemic because financial support was available from the government during the coronavirus crisis. Our services are going to be even more important in terms of helping our clients think about the consequences of increased utility bills and all of the other challenges that we might see in terms of revenue dips, higher material costs, supply glitches and so on.

From Digital to Human Firm, closing the client-centric circle

In 2007, I decided to create my firm with the idea that there must be a better way for accountancy firms to serve their clients. That started with how we presented and priced ourselves, with communication and transparency. With high expectations of the internet, I thought there had to be a better way – accounting software or technology on the internet – that would give us 24/7 access to our clients' data, that would help me provide myself and others with the services, (and prices), I wanted for myself.

Our move into cloud accounting allowed us to rethink the model. What we learned, warts and all, is recorded in The Digital Firm. In it, I took you step-by-step through what is required to become a fully digital accounting firm step. The Digital Firm is still relevant today. You can't become a human firm until you are properly digital. Meanwhile, we've learned a lot . We've more than doubled in size. This book shares that evolution, the short cuts and how to avoid our mistakes.

Let's look at accounting with a longer term view. Because when examined in the context of the last twenty to thirty years, what I am suggesting may look revolutionary. When considered as part of the continuum of accounting history it's something between a no-brainer and 'same story different tune'.

The Digital Firm
My previous book summarised what I learned during our leading-and-occasionally-bleeding-edge adoption of the best tech available to become a fully digital accounting firm. I refer to it regularly in this book, when building on a theme, comparing changes or expressing frustration.

The crisis doesn't change what we should be doing. If anything it emphasises the importance of our need to become more human-centric. And the points I covered five years ago still hold, only more so:

- New disruptive organisations have entered the accounting market. Not just accountancy firms using new tech to provide greater value services, but the tech companies themselves. These new players are focusing on where the opportunity exists in terms of using tech effectively, supporting clients who think differently and highlighting opportunities that may traditionally have been provided by traditional accounting firms.

More on this in Chapter 13, **Client Lifetime Value**

- While we are still waiting for MTD in its entirety, (whatever it's called, whatever that entails, whenever it happens ... because it will), its requirements for small businesses are here to stay. Firms that haven't taken this into account will inevitably have inefficiencies reducing their competitiveness and profitability.

More on this in Chapter 2, **The Engagement Correlation**

- Covid forced firms to implement work from home regimes. While this proves that firms can make change quickly when required, those that have adopted tech to enable home working as a knee jerk reaction, and did not consider their processes, work flow or training metrics will have compounded inefficiencies, reduced profitability and competitiveness.

More on this in Chapter 6, **Business, Marketing and the Mindset of Nice** and Chapter 14, **Making It Human**

- Millennials, Gen Z and Gen Alpha will form over 75 per cent of the workforce and a sizeable proportion of clients by 2025. They bring different expectations, lifestyle priorities and attitudes to work and life that can not be met by traditional firms.

More on this in Chapter 14, **Making It Human**

- It still takes manual accounting operations more than double the time of those using technology combined with properly considered processes.

More on this in Chapter 6, **Business, Marketing and the Mindset of Nice** and Chapter 22, **Too Much Noise**

- Capturing and gathering of the type of timely data that is easy for modern tech, bookkeeping and accountants to maintain, enables the offering of a new range of flexible advisory services.

  More on this in Chapter 6, **Business, Marketing and the Mindset of Nice** and Chapter 14, **Making it Human**

- Having taken the opportunity to demonstrate added value during the pandemic, clients have more expectations and firms more opportunities to deepen their client relationships. MTD and future potential requirements provide us with a framework within which we can do just that.

  More on this in Chapter 16, **The Point of Touchpoints** and Chapter 14, **Making it Human**

Change is ever more pressing than it was, and with it comes opportunity.

Accounting – a 7,500 year recap

The origins of accounting can be traced to around 7,500 years ago, when some bright spark used small clay counters to keep track of goods in ancient Mesopotamia. The idea caught on and many others followed. Auditing systems were recorded by early Egyptians and Babylonians, bookkeeping had emerged by 2000 BC and the Romans collected and collated extensive financial data.

The first bookkeeping reserve was published by Friar Luca Pacioli in 1494. Early adopters took his suggestions up quickly, and his ideas became the accountant's standard. By the end of the 1800s, investments were no longer games of knowledge or luck but considerations of risk and reward based on formal reports created or reviewed by impartial professionals who soon left their association with solicitors to create their own professional bodies, the first of which was ICAS, (the Institute of Chartered Accountants in Scotland), in 1854. William Pitt the Younger levied the first income tax and as other countries followed, the people needing specialist expertise grew. Individuals set up to service them, and as more and more large companies and corporations grew so did the accountancy profession.

Still getting new clients through word of mouth, by meeting in clubs, at golf, and at social events, in their drive to provide better personal service, accountants were amongst the first users of commercial adding machines, and then computers. It wasn't all plain sailing, but whether services were based on Pitt the Younger's income tax, the need for independently verified values for investors, adding machines, the advent of computers, leaders in the accountancy field seized once-in-a-lifetime opportunities and those who did not follow were eventually lost or subsumed.

Fast forward to today. Disasters such as Bernie Madoff, Carillion, Enron, Lehman Brothers, Patisserie Valerie, Saytam and Ted Baker led to new legislation, regulation and approaches. Our attention – quite naturally – shifted to compliance accounting and keeping our clients out of jail, but our relationships with clients got lost. Changes brought on by the challenges of tech, by HMRC's building towards a new regulatory regime that will effectively penalise practices that have minimal cloud adoption, new generations' priorities, the global pandemic and cost of living crisis mean more change for clients and firms. Innovators and newcomers have provided accounting services along new paradigms.

And while as accountants we all grumble about change, we always adapt to it and deal with it. In this context we can see that those firms able to change promptly profited greatly, later adopters survived and those who didn't fell by the wayside. Take-up on full digitisation has been so low that today's firms still have the early adopter advantage, which is bonkers! Meanwhile, waiting for MTD to stabilise will mean losing the competitive edge while making it harder to demonstrate compliance for any new conduct risk requirements.

More on this in Chapter 23,
Agile Visions and Lifetime Value to Future Proofing

> **MTD**
> MTD, (Making Tax Digital), was the catch-all name given to the UK Government's plan to have compliance data communications completely digital. Postponed, (and likely to be renamed when revived), HMRC's eventual goal still is to have all business transactions recorded as close as possible to the time when the transaction occurred. Eventually, quarterly reports, (as opposed to annual reports), will be required. This is part of a worldwide movement to digitise tax collection, and governments everywhere are reforming burdensome tax compliance procedures. Costa Rica, Indonesia, Malaysia, Peru, Vietnam and Zambia are among the first to have adopted systems with some automated features and Brazil appears to be one of the leaders in digitising tax compliance.

Bonkers!

"

Anybody can replicate, should they choose, the processes that successful digital firms are using, so the only way we can differentiate is the soft stuff – the human stuff – the way we engage with people, whether clients, colleagues, staff or contractors.

"

While our firm has evolved, people are still asking me about The Digital Firm's contents. When writing the book I was very much of the opinion that more firms would take on full digitisation. I was clearly ambitious for the profession because things didn't pan out. Anybody can replicate, should they choose, the processes that successful digital firms are using, so the only way we can differentiate is the soft stuff, the way we engage with people, whether clients, colleagues, staff or contractors but I still can't see that even 20 per cent of UK firms are truly digitally enabled. The numbers are still tiny. It is astonishing to think that 12 to 13 years on from when we first started doing this stuff that full digitisation is still the territory of early adopters, firms who – like us – moved swiftly on. The opportunity inherent in full digitisation is still huge, but many accountants are still doing things the same old way despite brand new technology acquisitions.

More on this in Chapter 11, **In The Numbers**

Still about the people, closing the circle

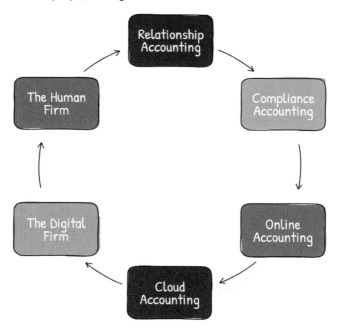

Not too long from now, tech will even out the playing field. Then the only way in which we will be able to differentiate an accountancy firm is by what we can do for our clients. To provide such services takes regular excellent communication. As a first step, and crucial to the development of a fully digital, fully human firm, we have brought client relationships back and made them central to our practices.

More on this **everywhere!**

We are not the only firm to close the historical circle and formally bring client relationships back where they should be. And while it has taken us all about 30 years to close the client-centric circle, the nature of our relationships with clients are different. New tech, new ways of communication and even new accounting approaches increase our ability to gather better data, which means we can surface better and more timely insights to enable our clients to thrive. Meanwhile, now we are able to advertise, (amazingly, our associations and coordinating bodies only gave permission in 1985), we are more accessible, which means more people can learn about us as we can get the message of our services and insights to a far more diverse range of people through online marketing, conferences and more. It's no longer about cosy relationships at exclusive clubs. We now have the data to deliver incredible value, and can deliver that quality to more than the people we just happen to meet.

``

> *The only thing that will differentiate an accountancy firm is what we can do for our clients.*

"

Back to the Future – Conversation with Sam Mitcham of SJCM Accountancy

Sam's practice has always been all about the client.

"I feel like I came into the industry at a very interesting time. I mean I'm nearly 34 now and I've been in this career since leaving school. When I first started as an accountant, relationships were central, and those relationships were very, very tight, so I've witnessed the fact that nobody really switched accountants, you know, unless the client passed away or stopped trading. From day one the relationship between the client and the partner that was in charge of that client was something that intrigued me. I knew from very early on in my career that was the bit I wanted in on, that year-end meeting. That's all it was then, you know, unless it was a really big client, with several check-in points. Generally, it was just that year-end meeting with not much contact throughout the year.

I knew that year-end meeting was where I wanted to be, so I could meet the client and learn about them. So straight away in my career I was asking; "Can I sit in on that meeting?" It took a couple of years, but eventually, the partner who started the firm that I was working for at the time would let me sit in. I remember him saying to me; "I've never had an apprentice ask to sit in on this meeting. Sam is it not boring for you? Because you probably have no idea what we're talking about?" But I loved it. Although he was right, a lot of the conversation went way over my head, I enjoyed it because – unbeknown to me at the time – I was witnessing a relationship there, a bond and a trust that had been formed over many, many years between that partner and that client. The partner wasn't doing the leg work, but the relationship was there. The communication piece was the bit that really intrigued me, because during that meeting you wouldn't just hear about the business, you'd hear about the wife and the kids and everything else that was going on in the client's life. That felt really important.

When people say accountancy is boring. I'm like; "You have no idea what we get to find out, on top of the finances. How can that be boring!"

Years later I saw the shift. Yes, technology was coming in. We had live data. We were doing cost and management accounts, we were having more regular check-in points. But I witnessed that shift between human and computer. At the year end point there might still be quite a lengthy email, and sometimes a year end meeting, but actually nine times out of ten it was a bit of a given, like; "This is your tax bill, and here are a few KPIs that the computer has generated and turned into a pretty graph."

And I noticed that clients were leaving the firm because they felt unloved. They were leaving because they felt like a number. They felt like they were part of a computer driven, technologically advanced process. They appreciated that they could start seeing the beauty of the automation and having the live data, but the human element was disappearing. So when I got to the point of starting my firm, I didn't have the finances behind me to go 'Boom!' right away but that suited me. I had to take it slow, but doing that has helped that relationship building that I wanted again with the clients.

So, of course I have all the tech. You know, my app stacks probably look as average as the next modern accountant's app stack. But I know about my clients. My clients know a bit about me. We sit down face to face. We have those meetings, and what I'm trying to kind of replicate is back when I was 18 or 19 and seeing that relationship. I'm trying to replicate that with the beauty of cloud technology."

Will to learn – the penny drop moment

I first looked at ReceiptBank in early 2010, and I didn't get it. Why put your receipts into an envelope, send them to ReceiptBank for them to scan it? I thought they were doing my job for me and wrote them off. A year later they launched the app. That was a game changing moment. I could give clients the app on their phone and all they had to do was photograph the receipt. That meant we were getting the data at the point they were spending the money, so long as we educated the client right. Eventually, I didn't have to chase clients monthly for receipts, and didn't have to sit in their office to do their bookkeeping, enabling us to build a bookkeeping offering that gave us control of the data. From there it was easy to tie up the fundamentals. The very basic minimum of doing cloud accounting was having a cloud General Ledger (GL) and an integrated pre-accounting tool. We no longer had to chase the data. If you're using a cloud GL and no pre-accounting tool, you're already wasting your time.

The take-home

Historically, accountants have maintained regular and excellent communications with their clients, adopting – and sometimes creating – new ideas and techniques with which to better serve them. At the time of writing this book, fewer than 20 per cent of UK firms have become fully digital. Fewer still are using the tech in a way that empowers their clients and encourages deeper mutual communication. This recent stalling of progress – at a time when I, for one, expected rapid sectoral change – is possibly a result of our focus on keeping clients out of jail rather than on maintaining a relationship. It's time to change that, to use the available technology to deepen and future proof our businesses and that of our clients. If you have decided to do that, this book is for you.

Help your clients; exceed their expectations.
Show you care, to generate value for all

2

Engagement Correlation

THEN

"Keep doing what you're doing to build engagement. Interest. Questions. Noticeability."

NOW

"Everyone is doing marketing, writing blogs ... We're creating greater expectations in our marketing so the importance of delivery is more critical. The focus now is about how we retain clients."

Keeping clients out of jail is no longer enough. As compliance requirements increase or change, we need to turn the additional associated costs of accountancy services into something that generates value. We can do this by finding things that provide additional value – real value – to our clients. We need to help them make the right business decisions as a normal, regular part of communications within the end-to-end process.

Recognising that we need to extend our thinking from purely meeting compliance requirements means that we need to extend our focus. When helping firms think about how to do this, I talk about the warm fuzzy feeling you can give a client if you show them you are really listening and thinking about what they need. A useful starting point is to ask how you – as a firm – want to make somebody feel.

I was talking about this recently to a bunch of new Farnell Clarke starters. It's a case of thinking about the effect of what we do as a firm on other people. Does it make them feel safe and secure? Is it balanced? Does it give them confidence to do something that they were unsure about? Does it increase their confidence because they know somebody has their back? Does it help the client feel that they are in control? Is it just making them feel that they are on the receiving end of somebody who really cares? Any kind of reaction that either takes away negativity or enhances positivity is great.

"

When you consider it, the idea of accountants making people feel really good is quite an alien concept.

"

How do you get the client to have a warm and fuzzy reaction to the things you do? You get it because you make people feel safe, secure, empowered and considered. Thinking through how to make clients feel good informs the way we think about how we engage with clients to get those kind of outcomes.

Back when we first started out, clients would post on social media that they never knew it could be so exciting going to the accountant. That's the kind of deep client experience we want to provide. We want to make people feel really good. When you consider it, the idea of accountants making people feel really good is quite an alien concept.

That feeling can be provided by lots of different things. They all elicit different kinds of positive emotions and demonstrate clearly why we need to focus on the human person, and how we make them feel good about what they are doing in their lives and in their businesses.

What is a touchpoint
A client touchpoint is any time a client or potential client interacts with your brand, whether that's through an employee or representative, a referer or referee, a process, a website, a social media post or interaction, an advertisement, or an app. The way we measure client experience is through the sum total of every client touchpoint. It's every way that a customer interacts with us.

Will to learn – nine lives
Back when we were a relatively new firm I often thought we had nine lives. We were growing and learning with our clients, as we worked out how to give them what I had envisaged. Sometimes we didn't get it right, but the relationships we had with our clients were so strong I was able to explain, and they'd be fine. Having those deeper relationships with our clients made me feel confident we could bounce back. If we made mistakes we could deal with them. These days I use the flip side to introduce the idea that if your client relationships aren't strong, your firm's resilience will suffer.

Son of MTD

We shouldn't rely on MTD, or any similar initiatives outside of the UK, to become more competitive. But it is a useful way to illustrate how client touchpoints can develop.

In 2018, when MTD was first introduced, I said HMRC had given us a once-in-a-lifetime opportunity to increase the number of touchpoints we have with clients. Now, in 2023, HMRC is re-creating that opportunity. Yes, there are challenges. The time has to be billed, so we need to work out how to provide more value. We need to consider how we can use the opportunity to deliver better data and greater insights. This is not about meeting the compliance requirements, because that is a given. It is about working out how we can use the opportunity to deliver real value.

The increase in client engagement is certainly greater because of the proposed quarterly requirements around MTD. Although it's on the back burner it is expected – probably – in 2026. How we might reassure clients directly on MTD is still nebulous. It is a regulatory requirement that is likely to drive changes in the way we operate, and we still don't know the full story other than there is likely to be more that we need to do for our clients. Having said that, there is reassurance in simply saying "hey, we've got this, there is this new legislation coming along, we are going to have to report to HMRC more regularly and we will take care of that for you in the best possible way". To simply do that, though, would be doing less for our clients than is possible. Better would be to consider that we need to be using the HMRC requirements as a reason to deliver something more than just ticking a box to say that the client has filed six times a year (or whatever it turns out to be).

Client Experience is more than just touchpoints

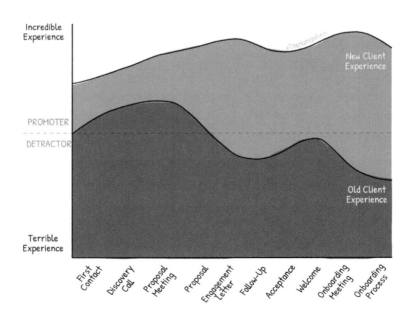

Blame it on HMRC (still)

So, how do we use the opportunity that has been created for us to make a difference to the client? We can look at how we might help them in terms of better business decision making. By doing this we can turn an external compliance requirement into a(nother) once-in-a-generation opportunity to fundamentally change what we do and how we do it. And the best part of this is, since we have to talk to the client anyway, even though it is mostly delayed, we can still blame it on HMRC!

So, the next opportunity – the evolution of competitive advantage – is all about people. And this is a longer term point of differentiation. While everyone can go and use Microsoft, Google or the same GL app, the human side of our work is always going to be unique. Human interactions must be key, and if we let technology be the key point of our focus, the value of human interactions and the opportunity involved in touchpoints becomes pointless. You find yourself in a race to the bottom because if it's not about people, it's about doing everything as cheaply, efficiently and impersonally as you possibly can.

There's no denying that the market dynamics are changing in terms of client expectations. Increasingly better informed, they are subjected to numerous adverts, and have a different outlook on life and work. Some tech providers will continue to encroach on low-value clients with seductive advertisements that imply no accountant is necessary if clients only use their apps. With no choice left, firms are forced to change. It's clear that in the not-too-distant-future, pure compliance services will be delivered cheaper – if not better – by the tech itself.

When our relationships with people become our key differentiator, our business is harder to replicate. This is back to basics, as described in the mini history of accounting on p20, but there's a difference. As practitioners of a more diverse, accessible and open service profession, we need to find the best ways to interact with, understand and suggest options to our clients, where necessary anticipating their needs. And with people – and relationships – becoming our differentiator, to ensure the creation and maintenance of excellent client relationships we need to look forward and design the kind of processes that facilitate early identification of insights and added value services based on the kind of timely data that has never been seen before.

Back to the future –
Conversation with Helen Cockle, COO of Futrli by Sage

In a wide ranging conversation about insights, marketing, the media and more, Helen said; "Firms' clients see the adverts about cash flow in the media and they do their research. They are being self educated. So there could be a real disconnect with what they will ask for and what they get, and whether they move to get it. I guess in theory [some] accountants are hoping that they'll just be asked for it [new insights/information]. But that creates a problem. These days people don't ask. They just Google."

"

> *There was a direct correlation between frequency of engagement and client satisfaction.*

"

During the pandemic, the accountants I spoke to said they were getting far more positive feedback than they would normally. I questioned them about what they thought was driving it and they responded that they were contacting clients more frequently to talk about the government support and associated benefits.

That was the point. There was a direct correlation between frequency of engagement and client satisfaction. The fact that they were going out to clients every two weeks and saying, "oh the government has now said this about furlough," and, "now you can apply for this loan" was raising their profile and improving their client relationships.

But they were being fed things to talk to their client about. It made them proactive because they didn't have to do the thinking. The government kept saying, "here's some new stuff," "here's some free money," so accountants saw it as their role to talk to clients about the free money. That drove greater conversations.

There is a direct link. The more we talk to clients, the happier they are likely to be about the things we can do. Luke Millar of Farnell Clarke gave me his perspective; "As we entered lockdowns and the effects of Covid hit clients, their priorities shifted as they looked to navigate the unknown. They played a more active role, contacting us regularly. Meanwhile, with real time data, our knowledge, and the various government schemes, we could provide our clients with proactive advice with the aim of taking stress away from them. Our clients have remained in frequent contact since."

The natural extension to all of that is to ask ourselves; when the government stops giving us things to discuss with our clients every two weeks, what are we going to do? What reason can we find to pick up the phone? What services and options can we talk to clients about? What can we build that will put us in a position where we are proactively going out to our clients on a regular basis?

Habitually good habits

By building client touchpoints into your processes the communication happens without the government feeding us new developments that we promptly need to discuss with our clients.

Daily bookkeeping is the obvious service opportunity to enable that to happen. While we encourage the habit of daily bookkeeping, we position it to clients as a weekly service, because the last thing they want is us chasing them every single day for every single receipt. This weekly service gives us the regular touchpoints that help build a deeper mutual relationship, one that we know – from pandemic experience – will be appreciated. More than this, it fulfils an obligation.

A professional obligation

One of the things we had a bit of a debate about in a recent Round Table was when I said I thought we had an obligation as accountants to help our clients understand the things they need, as well as what the client wants. I believe our obligation sits naturally with an accountant because as accountants, we really care. We want to make a difference. We want to help our clients in whatever way we can. If we've seen an opportunity in our accountancy practices to run better businesses, that extends to our obligation to help our clients use tech to run better businesses.

Do we have an obligation to give clients what they need as well as what they want? I believe we do. However that statement may be challenged by some accountants who might say that they are engaged to produce a set of accounts and a tax assessment. That reflects a different mindset and purpose.

When I bounced the round table conversation off Chris Downing, Director for accountants and bookkeepers at Sage, he said;

"I believe that as professionals we have a moral obligation to help all our clients. However, we've been traditionally reactive rather than proactive in our approach, possibly lacking the capacity to spend quality time with and better appreciate our clients' needs. In reality though, we can identify key themes that are common to every business, such as; I want to raise an invoice, I want to get paid faster, I want to be better organised, I want to be up to date on my taxes, I want to ensure my staff are happy. All of these are made better with the use of the right technology, and business owners want to explore what's available. But they don't know how to explore. I know from either speaking with clients or from people I know personally, there is a [genuine] lack of awareness of what is out there."

> **Will to learn – what client care means**
> Accountants have always cared about their clients. But if they only talk to them once a year what does that mean? Going beyond good service to great experience is more than building and maintaining relationships with clients so you keep them. It's as true for the business as it is for the person. You can't help people you don't know.

The importance of daily bookkeeping – Conversation with Kenji Kuramoto, Founder and CEO of Acuity

A recent conversation with Kenji Kuramoto emphasised the need for good quality data, and how that springs from daily bookkeeping. You can read more in the appendix.

"When I founded Acuity about 18-years ago, the mission at that point was to go and serve high growth innovative entrepreneurs with their accounting financial function. Specifically, the way that we were doing that was providing advisory services. A lot of CFO level services initially, but we always had a heart for helping small businesses and entrepreneurs. We identified rather quickly that doing the accounting – doing financial work – was their single least favourite job. There was not a single entrepreneur out there that said, "Oh, I can't wait to do my own, accounting and do my own financial work," as part of becoming an entrepreneur. So we wanted to step in and fill that gap and help them. We launched in Atlanta, Georgia, here in the United States, with all of our team members working in-market.

In our small universe, we were really grateful when we saw the emergence of cloud technologies. Fortunately for our firm, our number one client base has always been the technology companies, software companies. So, just by the fact that we serve software companies, we are immersed in tech. Our clients expect us to use tech. So, when we started seeing little bits of innovation in the accounting space we realised there was plenty of possibility.

Almost 10-years ago, we embraced the idea we could expand that market beyond just Atlanta. We thought, 'well, we don't have to get on site to their physical office. Through a cloud platform we can get in and serve clients anywhere'. So we started developing a greater depth of services alongside the recognition of the emergent cloud software.

We moved from being just a CFO advisory firm all the way down into bookkeeping. Some of our CFOs on the team and friends of mine who were Big Four looked at me like I was crazy and said, "why in the world do you want to go do bookkeeping? That's just the lowest level work!". To be fair, I also was not very sure about this. I thought, "wait a minute, I myself am a Big Four alumuni. I've been CFO of a tech Company. Why am I interested in bookkeeping?" But we saw so many challenges not going down that road. When the underlying data wasn't good we couldn't get to our higher level advisory work. We just couldn't do it because the underlying data wasn't sufficient to build financial models or pro-forma models or even to give sound advice to an entrepreneur.

I think it was our decision to move into more transactional level accounting and bookkeeping along with the emergence of the cloud solutions, that put us on the path. That's why we saw our growth really take off. Before that time we'd been growing as a firm by adding a few new controllers or new CFOs per year. We had just grown bit by bit, probably in a much more traditional professional services firm model. Just in the same way as in an accounting firm you'd maybe add a new partner or someone would be promoted to manager. We saw a very different type of growth that was built around the emergence of cloud technologies."

The take-home

Unless you are aiming for a low-cost-one-size-fits-all-dive-to-the-bottom firm you need to find ways to add value that are part of everyday processes. Since these days people will go elsewhere to find services if they don't know you provide them, this makes establishing client touchpoints even more important. The best way to establish regular touchpoints is to make them part of an existing process, and that process should include top quality, timely data.

Cheap or different?
There's not really a choice

3

Difference is Beautiful

THEN

"For as long as we focus on selling commodities, our primary focus will be price sensitive."

NOW

"It is an accountant's obligation to provide the best possible service to their client, so what is the problem?"

It's nothing new. It's really quite simple. If you don't want to be the cheapest, you've got to be different. And these days it is much harder to be different.

Farnell Clarke spent ten years focusing on the idea of technology being a differentiator. Nowadays, everyone can use that tech, and if they want they can copy our processes. We know this, so while we have benefitted massively from technology being our differentiator so far, we know we have to keep thinking about what will differentiate us in the future. If we have to keep thinking, other firms are going to have to keep thinking too.

Before the advent of the internet as we know it, accountants found new business through word of mouth, in clubs, playing golf or socialising, making the individual's personality and presence imperative. Our accountancy institutions and associations required us not to advertise, so indirect business development was the only way.

In those times a firm was differentiated by the personal relationships its partners had with others. Limited by the strictures of their associations and institutions, and the general business environment, they pretty much always looked the same, did the same and charged around the same.

We've come full circle, having moved away from relationship accounting to concentrate on compliance, tech and the cloud has enabled a new human-centric approach

I've always said that we should focus firmly back on client relationships and touchpoints. Since the market dynamic is no longer determined by the old-world in-club development of personal relationships, no longer is the relationship of a firm's partners with its clients outside the office a sufficient differentiator. Although there is still a value in those relationships, for most firm's it's no differentiator at all. The market dynamic has changed to how we present ourselves online, in the global shop window and to where people can compare our personal relationships to the messages we portray online.

It is easier than ever for us to present ourselves in different ways, harder to be seen to be different. This differentiation is compounded since some of the tech companies are using big advertising budgets to present themselves as providing holistic tech solutions, leading some potential clients to think they are more than just tools to simplify the accounting process. Some particularly optimistic microbusiness startups may misguidedly interpret this as a total solution, believing they don't need an accountant or bookkeeper.

Even when we establish and articulate our key differences, it is hard to demonstrate them in everything we do. However, by making sure our differences are unique differences that have naturally arisen from our purpose, vision and values, in our communications we can rise above the throng. People, being instinctively different, produce genuine, authentic differences which can't be rivaled by tech, and makes this task slightly easier.

Porter's strategies for competitive advantage

In his book *Competitive Advantage,* (The Free Press, 1985), Michael Porter suggests four generic categories by which you can attain competitive advantage. Considering how to differentiate your firm in terms of Cost Leadership, Differentiation, Cost Focus and Differentiation Focus and their respective sub-divisions an organisation can make strategic choices in terms of developing and maintaining competitive advantage.

Porters Strategies for Competitive Advantage (the Free Press, 1985)

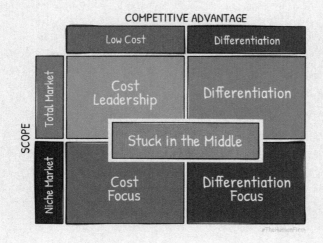

Will to learn – wrong number

Back in 2018, I estimated that 20 per cent of firms in the UK were either doing cloud accounting or moving towards the fully digital firm, and only two per cent fully digital. It's bonkers that so few firms aren't on their way to being fully digital by now. It means there are still significant opportunities for firms that can swiftly become fully digital on the way to becoming Human Firms. Those in that top 20 per cent today are still in the top quartile. If we accept the number there is still an early adopter advantage to be had.

❝

Marketing on the same message.

❞

You'll read similar claims on so many websites. You'll find all the right terms on their web pages. Look deeper though, because while many have the ability to offer cloud software, that doesn't mean they are fully digital. Providing online or cloud-based options was part of the story five years ago when I wrote the Digital Firm, and is even less of the story now. Irrespective of the fact that their reality may be somewhat different, it leaves us marketing on the same message.

Put aside the fact that, since a lack of fully integrated automation will inevitably cost the firm more, (as we saw in The Digital Firm), the regulatory regime to which, (if you are a glass-half-full person), HMRC will eventually introduce, effectively penalises firms that have not become fully digital.

❝

Becoming a fully digital firm whilst living and breathing our distinctive competencies, is no longer enough.

❞

We can easily envision a point at which everybody has access to the same technology, (or different technology providing the same functions). Everybody will then be able to provide similar processes and team structures. That alerts us to look for further opportunity, and the next evolution of an accountancy firm's competitive advantage. Becoming a fully digital firm whilst living and breathing our distinctive competencies, is no longer enough.

Key words can be both used and misused by firms . . .

. . . and by clients

Consider deeply how the firm manifests and displays what you present on your website. This includes consistent behaviour with existing and potential clients and staff, as well as differentiating your product offering. (Farnell Clarke includes digital marketing, digital savvy people, a consistent internal and external digital approach).

For now, firms can succeed through clearly communicating their integrated digital approach, which is a combination of people, process and technology, (built upon the cloud-based approach discussed in my previous book). However, to maintain their competitive advantage they need to live it, breathe it, demonstrate it, and go beyond it. This takes us back to relationships, touchpoints and people, and what this book is about.

> **Keeping considerations clear**
> When I say 'focus on the client', it's always about the individual relationship that a firm has with a client. When I talk about 'clients', plural, that is about the experience we deliver. It's important. By keeping very focused on what we are considering, we can work on how best to serve ... the client.

Value in articulating value

Developing an explicit client and employee value proposition is pretty new for Farnell Clarke, although we had a subconscious view of what we needed. Articulating both sides makes it clear about what our offer is. Whether it's about staff understanding our proposition to our clients, or our clients understanding how we work with our team, this is a really valuable step.

> **The CVP (Client Value Proposition)**
> CVP is a statement that defines the unique benefit a product or service provides to its customers. It outlines the specific needs and wants of the customer and how the product or service meets those needs better than competitors. It communicates the value the firm offers to its clients and sets expectations for the client experience.

The EVP (Employee Value Proposition)

An EVP is the unique set of benefits and rewards that the firm offers its employees in exchange for their skills, experience and performance. It outlines the value that the firm provides to its employees including compensation, benefits, work-life balance, professional development, company culture and in our case, the pub.

The CVP, (Client Value Proposition), and EVP, (Employee Value Proposition), are articulations of what we do and how we do it. The CVP clearly articulates what we want to do for our clients while the EVP gives clarity to the team exactly what we are saying we will do for them, and how we will do it.

It goes without saying that the two must be aligned. By developing strong CVP and EVP we differentiate ourselves from our competitors in the eyes of both our clients and employees.

Farnell Clarke's Current CVP

"Farnell Clarke provides our clients with a high-touch, technology-driven, people first, finance and tax compliance and advisory service. Our unique approach ensures our clients:

- Get valuable and timely advice when they need it,
- Have the support they need to meet their business and personal goals,
- Are free from time consuming accounting and tax activities allowing them to focus on what they do best,
- Know that we are in their corner and a truly integrated part of their team.

We deliver this through our best in class client experiences that is delivered by our unique ability to perfectly blend the right people, following the right process, utilising the right technology. A digital driven mindset that has been developed and refined consistently since 2007."

A recent conversation I had with Rob Brown from Accounting Influencers gives another perspective on how we might usefully articulate value. Here is part of what he said;

"There are many accountants that make claims and are never held accountable for them. The claims win the client, the claims win the candidate, win the employee and once they're in, the accountant is not necessarily held to account for the claims they made.

That's where I see the edge and the next level of pioneering. Most pioneers end up face down, in the dirt, with arrows in the back, because it's not accepted by the marketplace. You're almost too radical for what people are ready for. But the next level on, from what you're saying, is to give evidence for your points of differentiation.

So beyond what you're copying and claiming from anyone else, beyond what you're replicating and duplicating from other websites, whether intentionally or inadvertently, clients and candidates will become more and more discerning and will ask, "Well, are they really doing this?" Then it becomes a point, a question of proof, and you need to become an accountant that doesn't just claim it, you do it. And not only are you doing it for real, but then you have evidence. As Muhammad Ali said, it ain't bragging if you've done it.

In the old world, proof came from old-style testimonials and case studies. But the new world of proof in the video world that we live in is documented proof; video case studies and video testimonials and video stories from people saying what a difference you've made, and saying how what you're claiming is true.

For instance, I spoke to a managing partner of a mid-tier firm, and I asked him, "what's different about your firm?" And he said, "we have a zero overtime policy". And I said, "what does that look like?" And he said, "the average overtime for everyone in our firm is 30 minutes a month". I said that can't be easy. It must create all kinds of capacity issues. I asked for an example of how that plays out. He explained that at 5.30pm every day he comes out of his office and walks around the floor, and if anyone's still there he asks them why. The implication is that employees should have gone home. He explained that some might have a legitimate reason for working late. Perhaps they came in late because of the school run, or they're taking Friday morning off, so they're working a little bit later. But if they are they're cramming in 10-hours a day, and doing that every day, then it needs to be addressed. There is an issue with the culture.

It's important that not only do they have that policy, but they are evidencing that they are living the policy by walking around implementing it. Telling that story with the managing partner, putting that on a video and putting that on the website or showing it to candidates, for me that's proving they are a human firm."

The take-home

- While many firms claim that they are fully digital, the truth is somewhat different. This leaves opportunity for firms converting to full digital now,

- There is still some time remaining whereby you can take early adopter advantage by living and breathing full digitisation (and by demonstrating this to staff and clients alike),

- Time is running out in which being a digital firm can be used as a differentiator. Everyone will end up with fully cloud-based systems, supported by similar processes. Becoming a fully digital firm – even whilst living and breathing our distinctive competencies is no longer enough alone to make us stand-out,

- To maintain competitive advantage, a firm must clearly understand its CVP (Client Value Proposition) and demonstrate it through all it does and says, and this CVP, while delivering on compliance, is about client centric facilitation and communications.

To recruit, retain,
and attract the best
clients and staff
we need to recognise
what they want

4

Generation Shift and Buying Behaviours

THEN

"Millennials and Gen Z, who will form over 70 per cent of the workforce and a sizeable proportion of clients by 2025, have a different set of expectations and lifestyle priorities that cannot currently be met by traditional firms."

NOW

"Business owners' expectations have increased. More recent generations' expectations are broader too, so we need to look at every aspect of what we do and how we do it and be more proactive."

Talkin' about generations

Generations and their cut-off points are not exact, and for some purposes can be considered to overlap. They are however, useful tools that provide a way to understand how different formative experiences, (world events, technological, economic and social shifts), shape people's views. While younger and older adults may differ in their views at a given moment, generational cohorts allow consideration of how older generations felt about a given issue when they themselves were young, as well as to describe how the trajectory of views might differ across generations. At roughly 16 years, (roughly 1981-1996), the Millennials age span is equivalent to

Generation X and their preceding generation (roughly 1965-1980). By this definition, (because others exist), both are shorter than the Baby Boomers span of 19 years, which is based on the famous surge in births after World War II and the significant decline of birth-rates after 1964. Dates for more recent generations – and even their names – are not yet stable.

Although not defined through exact science, a generation shift is a change in attitudes, habits and behaviours between the people of one generation and another. Douglas Adams wrote, "anything that is in the world when you're born is normal and ordinary and is just a natural part of the way the world works. Anything that's invented between when you're fifteen and thirty-five is new and exciting and revolutionary, and you can probably get a career in it. Anything invented after you're thirty-five is against the natural order of things," in Hitch Hikers Guide to the Galaxy. Lazlo Bock, Head of Human Resources for Google says the cycle repeats every ten to fifteen years.

Maisie, Millenials and more – Conversation with Maisie Poskitt, Head of Amazing at BHP LLP

I talked to Maisie about the research behind her report; 'Engaging and Training the Accountants of Tomorrow' and her answers were fascinating.

"I started by kind of getting them to describe where they were in their work and life. So, how long they had been working and what generation they fit into. Then I asked, well, the same questions, but I split down the data and picked out the GenZ answers, and the GenX answers, and so on and so forth. I got two branches of the survey, depending what answers had been picked in the beginning, so GenZ answered questions like, "what do you want to see in the future," and, "what do you like about work at the moment?" But what was actually more interesting I also asked the older people than GenZ who had answered the survey what they think GenZ wants. The answers were extremely different.

The older people said GenZ would put work-life balance at the top, with eco-tendencies like green initiatives; but what GenZ actually want primarily is very in line with what previous generations have wanted. I think that other generations are creating a GenZ mould. I want to call it the Greta Thunberg Effect. The most influential GenZ that we've got at the moment is probably Greta Thunberg. If you look at the news, and how they report on her compared to other people, she is labelled as GenZ, has become the archetype of the generation. But if you have others of the same generation, they are just given their name."

Our experience – and perceptions – are that there has been a big change in aspirations since the Millennials, but from her own research Maisie doesn't seem to agree.

"I don't think it has actually swayed as far as we think it might have done. I think there is a perception that Millennials were very different to the generations that have come before, but when you actually say to someone what is important to you? Here is a list, move what you want to the top and what you don't to the bottom, it does come out quite similar.

If you say to them, what do you want out of work, they're going to say work-life balance. I want a good salary. I want good progression. But if you say to them, do you not want job security too? They will say, "oh yes, I definitely want job security". And that leaps the top of the list. So I think, where my survey is concerned, because I gave a prescribed 16 items and asked them to order what was most to what was least important, it meant there wasn't that kind of open-endedness to the question. That meant that Millennials and GenZ wouldn't probably have been outliers, if you see what I mean, because they saw job security in front of them, and they thought, "that is quite important", so it went up close to the top, for all generational categories."

Generations, aspirations

Bizarrely, every generation has different aspirations, approaches and working practices. That said, there was something about the Millennial's generation shift that for me felt bigger and greater than the previous generational shifts. Others might argue that the Boomer to GenX was a huge shift as well, but that seems to me to have been more evolutional. It may be because I was more aware and more interested in what was going on with them. We have talked about how buying decisions are driven by values. As well as that, there was a feeling that work-life balance was more important, and an acceptance of the job for life having disappeared. In itself, that changes your mindset. If you know you are not going to be in the same job for life, you think differently about what you want to do and how you're going to do it.

So, while I think it's far too easy to stereotype a whole generation – because there are always exceptions and people are different – most of the research suggests that Millennials want a greater work-life balance. They make buying decisions based more on values than money. And while some say that Millennials are lazy and feel entitled, I don't think that is at all true. In the last book we had statistics indicating that around two thirds of all Millennials would leave their job within the next four years. When talking to accounting firm owners and partners I have used those statistics as a provocation, asking them to consider whose fault is that. Because it isn't the Millennials fault. It's our fault as employers.

If we want to recruit and retain the best people, we need to recognise each generation shift, that stuff changes in the world in which we operate and that people of different generations are looking for something different. We have to accept that the expectations of the people we want to employ are going to change. Consider the Millennials – people born largely between 1982 and 2000. They are the first generation of digital natives. The impact of new technology, all the influences on Millennials is compounded when we start considering Gen Z, (those born from the year 2000), the oldest of whom is 23 as I write.

Far more driven by vision and values, this growing proportion of business owners and senior managers are Millennials and GenZ. Expectations have increased and are broader so the only way we can meet them is through understanding them; which means talking to them. We need to look at every aspect of what we do and how we do it, be proactive in discovering and delivering on clients expectations, objectives and desires. Focus on service offerings that deliver true value.

Table showing attitudes and aspirations of the generations from Maturist to GenZ

CHARACTERISTICS	MATURISTS (pre-1945)	BABY BOOMERS (1945-1960)	GENERATION X (1961-1980)	GENERATION Y (1981-1995)	GENERATION Z (Born after 1995)
Percentage in UK workforce*	3%	33%	35%	29%	Employed part-time or in new apprenticeships
Aspiration	Home Ownership	Job Security	Work-Life Balance	Freedom & Flexibility	Security & Stability
Attitude toward technology	Largely Disengaged	Early tech adopters	Digital Immigrants	Digital Natives	"Technoholics" dependant on IT
Attitude toward career	Jobs are for life	Organisational - careers are defined by employers	"Portfolio" careers - Loyal to profession, not employer	Digital entrepreneurs - work with organisations, not "for"	Career multitaskers - will move easily between orgs and "pop-up" businesses

*Approximate at time of publication   #TheHumanFirm

Think about what has happened since 2000. The massive change around the way that we use and rely on technology. A Stanford study tells us GenZ are highly collaborative, self-reliant and pragmatic. They value diversity and finding their own unique identities. Combined with Millennials they create a shift in the way we all work and interact. And these are the people who are coming into our workforce. If we play our cards right they are also our newest cohort of clients. So again, we have to consider what do these generations really want, what are they striving for and what is important to them. Meanwhile everything else has got better so we really need to think hard about the way we offer our services and how they align with our clients and our staff alike.

"

> *While restricting your recruitment to people who are not one of the two demographics leaves you with little succession planning, limiting your clients in a similar way restricts your ability to build a good client base.*

"

While we need to avoid stereotyping a whole generation, to avoid hiring these people limits you to oldies like me. Whatever our personal attitudes – which may be much younger – these 'oldies' are at the latter end of GenX. That means they are 50 or even more, and may have an inability to adapt to new environments and requirements. That is likely to alienate clients and staff alike.

Particularly with GenZ the idea of digital entrepreneurs who work with – and not for – organisations, pulls into the debate around the gig economy. How should we build to enable choice for these people? Will they want that flexibility? Or is it necessity? Whichever is appropriate for your target clients, knowing this informs your behaviours and the services you offer. Similarly, Generation X's portfolio career structure and the way they move between employers requires another sort of thinking, product and service offering. The key message is that, like everything and everyone else, we have to be prepared to adapt, and to recognise the significant shifts in aspiration, work-life balance and thinking of different generations so that we can talk about what we can do to help each client.

Recognise that you need to make the most of your specific awareness of the buying behaviours and priorities of Millennials and more recent generations. Be clear that potential clients will look to see how you live your values and implicit in that is the way you consider and use recruitment as a marketing activity. Make sure your flexibility, vision, values and approach are clear throughout your recruitment and marketing material. Despite everything that has gone on with Covid, many firms have not adapted and are pulling back into old behaviours, so make sure that your marketing materials and your recruitment shows clearly that you are not. Make no mistake, Just as clients will recognise there is a better way to have their accounts managed and will head for the hills, our team members will do the same thing. If that happens, the firm will then find it extremely hard – if not impossible – to recruit staff of the quality they'd prefer.

The take-home

Life has changed hugely over the last few years. Digital natives take tech enablement for granted, don't expect jobs for life and have radically different values that inform their buying behaviour, business management style and their future plans. Both expectations and the broadness of these expectations have increased, so firms need to explicitly and actively understand the buying behaviours, expectations, desires, visions and values of more recent generations, to recruit people who relate to these generations and to understand that potential clients will choose based on how we live our values.

Don't get hung up on your logo, firm culture and personality count for more

5

The Living Brand

THEN

"Positioning ourselves for that market is not just a matter of branding – it transfers into everything else we do."

NOW

"Brand isn't enough. Everyone needs a strong brand. However, we need to go beyond brand to a fluid personality that reflects who we are, and that everyone understands."

I'm not a marketeer, but I firmly believe that confusing the idea of static conventional branding, such as that you see through consistent colours and logos, with inflexible delivery will eventually result in disaster. Life isn't static. Business isn't static. Accountancy isn't static. So creating a brand that's fixed, with messages that are planned and unchangeable within it makes no sense. A living brand provides strength and flexibility. The living brand, which comprises of the firm's personality, the brand personality, and conventional branding itself, enables a flexibility, firm-wide resilience and consistency of approach in an authentic statement that will be recognised and appreciated by clients, staff and stakeholders alike.

Not so typical, a very special firm

Back when I first started the business, people would ask what I did. I'd say "I'm an accountant, but I'm not your typical accountant". That became our strapline. Nowadays, everyone seems to use a version of this message. In marketing terms they have made themselves typical for being untypical. Meanwhile, we have moved away from that messaging entirely and are now continuously establishing our firm's brand at the deepest of levels. Before I share with you how we've done it, you need to understand the 'why'.

Encroachment is useful

Pilot.com is a US-based online provider of back-office accounting, CFO and tax services for startups and small businesses. While it does nothing more than many other forward thinking accountancy firms, it has a one billion dollar valuation, and Jeff Bezos has invested in it. The amount of cash they have available to spend on advertising is an indicator of the huge potential they see in the market and of an unprecedented level of perceived competition with many smaller firms.

In the US, Intuit launched QuickBooks Live along with heavily marketed associated accounting services. This service uses existing QuickBooks advisor communities to deliver Intuit's integrated software and bookkeeping. Looked at another way, because they are delivering extensive, (and expensive) marketing, they are able to bring previously independent accountants into 'approved' service providers while taking the primary client relationship away from them. Put aside the competitive aspects of this action, and you'll see massive marketing campaigns that highlight the importance of bookkeeping. Yes, providing we have the right people in the right place we can undertake the bookkeeping services just as efficiently and effectively, and that may be considered competition. But what we can do that Intuit can not, is deliver quality services, insights based on our close knowledge of our clients and a consistent, caring client relationship.

> **"**
> *As accountants we know it is not that simple, but knowing the fact*
> *without sharing it is no longer enough.*
>
> **"**

In the UK, a number of roll-outs of similar services have met varying degrees of success. The encroachment seems inevitable. The technology required for Son of MTD has enabled some tech companies to make the claim that small businesses can file their returns with their software, whilst GL solutions advertise how easy it is to do with their products too. As accountants we know it is not that simple, but knowing the fact without sharing it is no longer enough.

Meanwhile, other new firms – younger entrepreneurial accountants – are entering the market, clear in the knowledge that there is a better way, and happy to act on these newer ideas of what makes great accounting services themselves.

Porter's 'Five Forces' from Competitive Advantage

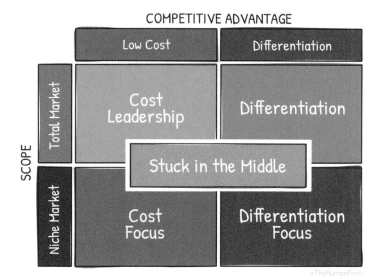

61

This – as you have probably recognised from earlier in the book – is a classic demonstration of the applicability of Porter's Strategies of Competitive Advantage. It contrasts competition for cost leadership, (I've already described that as a race to the bottom for all but a few), with the differentiation illustrated by the new-entrants' determination to provide what they believe is necessary through their own tech-enabled, tech-savvy, innovative processes.

These new players come to market with a clear focus on where their opportunity exists. They use tech effectively, think of servicing clients differently, and are themselves a different sort of client. A further illustration – should any more be needed – of why established firms are faced with new competition that manifests in loads of different ways. If they continue to bury their heads in the sand, and do nothing with regards to differentiating themselves, such competition will ultimately accelerate the old style pre-digital firms' demise.

What does brand mean to you?

In a recent round table, I asked the group what brand meant to them. In attending the round table they showed themselves as modern, open and progressive, and their answers were as varied as you'd hope.

"Google reviews."

"Our values and ethos and how we want to be perceived in the market."

"It has always been a bugbear for me. I don't feel that our institute promotes our brand. We're chartered accountants and the average person on the street still doesn't know what that is."

"On top of our brand, people ask me if I'm a chartered accountant. People look at my website to check I'm ACCA and my approach. Today's age of entrepreneurs are savvy and they may not tell you but they have checked you out, so putting out who you really are is important."

"Brand to me means everything. It literally has my name on it. That's me they are talking about. I want pride in my name. Although it was a lazy branding decision originally, I won't allow it to be awful."

"We're an all-female firm and want to be the most trusted advisor. We will be honest. We won't necessarily always have the right answer, but we know people who do. Even our IFA is female, as is our HR advisor. Referring someone to a chap in a pinstripe suit didn't work, we had to find someone like us."

Brand, living brand and personality

Establishing your brand in the conventional marketing sense, (the manner in which an organisation presents itself to the public), is a start, but by no means enough.

You hear marketeers talk about brand and its relationship with culture, but for me culture is still static. I've asked myself how we can have personality that's responsive to change, that's consistent with our brand and culture and that everyone can buy into. It's particularly important – and hard to create – when you start talking about multi-partner firms. Such firms have multiple personalities, nobody knows quite what the right personality is and navigating to a single consensus is likely to be a long and time-consuming process. It's important, nonetheless. Personality goes beyond brand because it is more fluid and can evolve.

Take Farnell Clarke's journey as an illustration. 15 years in, we are kind of coming out of our teenage years. We are growing up, having to be more serious and maybe not having fun in the way we used to. But we're not losing sight of who we are. We think hard about the personality that we portray. It comes back to things like the pub in our office. That's personality, not culture and not brand. It's a statement of who we are and what you can expect from us, an element of human consistency of vital importance.

Will to learn – Why do you do what you do

What I say to firms, (and if you know me, you know I say it a lot), is that we need to understand and articulate why they do what they do, what they do and how they do it. If they can, it gives them a clearly defined marketing message. It's really easy to grow an accountancy firm, (you need to know these things and articulate them effectively). While that enables you to grow, the challenge becomes how do you scale up.

Too many people get hung up on the concept of branding being what their logo looks like. Branding isn't the marketing message. There is a clear distinction. As part of this I often ask firms to write down the three things that make you unique, then look at your website and see if your website talks about them. The majority of firms do not.

Culture, brand personality and service

Company culture, brand and personality play a crucial role in shaping the services provided by an accounting firm. A strong company culture can help foster a positive work environment and promote teamwork, leading to higher job satisfaction and better performance from employees who are naturally more engaged. This engagement and employee happiness can in turn result in improved customer service, more creative approaches to delivering client insight and a more enjoyable experience for all.

Brand and personality, on the other hand, help establish the accounting firm's unique identity. The two together inform everything that people do, and sets the firm apart from its competitors. The personality communicates the values and expertise of the firm, building a strong emotional connection with its audience.

The values and beliefs embodied by the company culture also influences the way the firm acts and interacts with its clients. A culture that values transparency and honesty may lead to a more straightforward approach to client communication; a culture that prioritises innovation may use language and memes more appropriate to start-ups; and a culture that prioritises social impact may result in different comparisons, expertise and spread.

The importance of culture and brand personality extends further. We are seeing one of the biggest generational shifts ever, with remote working and work-life balance taking a greater priority in many people's lives. Many professional accountants are more interested in buying houses than into a firm, particularly one achieving single digit growth or one where the individuals believe they won't fit. Culture, brand personality and its communication – not through mere communications but by reputation and example – are therefore important in terms of succession planning as well as the bottom line.

Importantly, this should all be based on the 'why, what and how' I've already discussed.

What is important when client experience is key? Everything!

Will to learn – our big personality statement

We put a pub into our office in 2016. That's not a brand statement. It's a statement of our firm's personality. Of who we are. We know that some people won't want to work with an accountancy firm with a pub in their office. And that is fine. It combines with our branding, our vision and values and we wanted - and still want - clients who get that. Clients who get that we care about them and our staff, who understand our mission and like our approach.

But there's more... Once you have considered and integrated your conventional branding guidelines, you need to create something that isn't so static. I called it the living brand because it is not stationary anymore. Your brand – the way everyone perceives your organisation – has to be able to grow.

Conventionally, brand personality demonstrates the feelings that the brand itself should elicit: A company's brand personality inspires an emotional response in a specific consumer segment, with the intention of inciting positive actions that benefit the firm. There are five main types of brand personalities with common traits. They are excitement, sincerity, ruggedness, competence, and sophistication. Customers are more likely to purchase a brand if its personality is similar to their own.

"

Firm personality is a really powerful thing for firms to enact.

"

Firm personality goes deeper. While brands, (and brand personalities), are static, firm personalities adapt and flex. They reflect mood and respond to events in a way that is consistent with the branding, the intentions and the internal environment of the firm itself. Firm personality is a really powerful thing for firms to enact. Much stronger than mere messaging, it gives everyone in the firm the confidence that they're pulling in the right direction along with how they should be thinking, and everyone outside the firm the reassurance that the firm is authentic, clear in its aspirations and truly knows where it's at.

If you can not articulate who you are in a clear and understandable way throughout all of your enterprise, your team won't know who you are, your clients won't know who you are, and time, energy and goodwill will be spent as your firm and the people in it bumble through random responses to internal and external changes, rather than making decisive moves based on the understanding of who you really are.

Whether a one-person operation or huge operation, firm personality is an important thing to address. The explicit adoption of firm personality with larger traditional firms is a very hard thing to do. Comprised of partners, each of whom has become accustomed to imposing their own personality on their department, client group, vertical or horizontal market, such firms often present a split-personality to the outside world. While this may have worked well in the past, it is vital to resolve the multiple personalities of the partners to get firm personality right.

So, if you don't know who you are, your team won't know who you are and neither will your clients. And that's a problem. You can have this lovely brand that you put all over your website, but people still won't really know who you are because you are exhibiting a kind of mixed personality. However, if everybody can buy into a clear and consistent firm personality, and that personality is driven by and underpinned by purpose, vision and values, your firm personality powers – and empowers – your firm.

Will to learn – conscious communication

Far too often, people think a brand is just a logo. It's far more than that. So I decided that, if we rename it – if we call 'brand' something else – it might get people to focus on the whole concept in a way that doesn't unstick their thinking. That's why, a long time ago – in 2010 or 2011 – we spent some time thinking about the values that underpinned our brand and that would take us into our brand personality. This became a start point in an exercise we did with our entire team to get everyone to really think about what underpins our brand, and the values for which we want to be famous. We asked ourselves what are the things that we want everyone to buy into, and to understand. It worked well.

What worked less well was how we managed this as Farnell Clarke grew. It became a real challenge, because as new people joined and our teams grew, we didn't put enough work into the explicit awareness of our firm personality. As the directors stepped away from the day-to-day business, we forgot to communicate firm personality to new staff members and others. To an extent, it got lost. We've caught up with ourselves now, and are doing all kinds of things to re-embed this stuff into the team, into all levels of organisational development plans, and to really make sure we get back to the basics in terms of everybody understanding those values.

The lesson we learned here is don't lose sight of the fact that the Living Brand needs conscious communication, explicit integration and Firm-wide awareness. It's a fundamentally important way of ensuring consistency, empowering everyone and helping people understand how and why they should act.

The take-home

The Living Brand is more than logos and corporate colours. It includes a statement of firm personality – a deep articulation that enables people within the firm to know how to respond to different situations and that gives confidence of authenticity, consistency and character to people outside the firm.

Think more like a business
and less like an employee

6

Business, Marketing and the Mindset of Nice

THEN

"Every digital firm will find their services, products, marketing, sales and internal and external communications inextricably linked."

NOW

"As you can see when it comes to the big picture of marketing for the digital practice, it's (also) as much about changing our mindset, thinking more like business owners and less like accountants."

A nice call to conscience

Accountants are strongly motivated to do right by our clients. We are known for being a safe, steady and reliable pair of hands and want to help clients develop better, stronger, more competitive and resilient businesses. We like to help our clients, to be nice. What we're less good at is demonstrating our value, and charging for that extra little thing and saying to the client why we are doing so. We need to change that, it's important, so you'll read it again. If we have no experience of managing this type of pull, about the thinking and change involved in developing resilience how can we, in conscience advise others? Unless our own firms are stronger, more competitive and more resilient, and unless we are clearer at articulating value and difference, we can't help our clients as well as we'd like, and to provide quality services efficiently, effectively and at reasonable costs we need to be clear on those costs and ready to change.

> **"**
> *We no longer have a choice.*
> **"**

We no longer have a choice. Well, actually we do. We can continue to bury our heads in the sand, do nothing and inevitably, eventually fail.

That you are reading this book means you want to benefit from the transformation to a Human Firm. That means getting your firm to fully digital status as soon as possible if you haven't already. Only once you are a fully cloud-based, digitally enabled firm can you start properly considering the transformation to Human.

Mindset moulding

When I spoke to Stefan Barrett of Bee Motion he told me that he gave all his new starters the old Digital Firm book. He took his own path, but said that the core values, the mindset and the approach I set out was exactly what Bee Motion was built on. It's a wonderful compliment of course, and a great example of how he moulds the mindset of all new staff members of his firm.

The mindset of difference

How can every firm be different? Of course, there are lots of ways we can differentiate what we do; our brand, quality, our people, and so on. It starts with explicitly having a deliberate strategy to clarify how we will be different, and building a marketing plan to let people know. Before that it requires a mindset change.

When I set up Farnell Clarke back in 2007, I had no preconception about how to run an accounting firm but I had a clear purpose. Because of this I put myself in the shoes of a client and asked a simple question: "If I were a client of an accounting firm what would I want?"

This became the mantra for our firm as we grew. As much of the market had a prescribed approach on how to do what they did, it meant much of the competition was the same and had very little to differentiate them. This was largely because they were stuck in that old mindset. A cycle that prevented thinking outside of the box.

"

That old mindset. A cycle that prevented thinking outside of the box.

"

Without the years of baggage held by people running traditional firms I had a different mindset. I was able to think about how technology could change our offer. How a different approach to pricing and service delivery could allow us to stand out from the crowded market. A market where firms everywhere were offering broadly the same thing for a largely similar price. A willingness to try new things and be prepared to rethink the business model allowed us as a firm to operate at the 'bleeding edge' and lead the charge towards what is now largely standard practice in our sector. The results of your change of mindset need not be as radical as mine. You don't need to live on the bleeding edge, but changing it is important nonetheless.

I was speaking at a large event in the US back in 2019 when one of the speakers talked about digital disruption. He termed and positioned it perfectly for me. He said that, 'disruption is simply removing friction from the process'. Think about that carefully. Then think about all the things you do in every part of your business. Where is the unnecessary friction for your clients or your team? How can a rethink of your business approach change things for the better or remove that friction to create better client or customer experiences? A change of mindset is your best place to start.

The mindset of lifestyle –
Conversation with Eriona Bajrakurtaj,
MD of Majors Accounts

Eriona made a conscious decision to change. That's quite a challenge. I asked her to tell me about it, and this is some of what she said;

"In 2016 or 2017 I decided to start looking at the tech to be sure we would be compliant with MTD and Quickbooks invited me to QuickBooks Connect (QBC).

I went along thinking what am I going to gain from this? Because they were saying, "it's so great, you're going to have so much fun!" I'm like yeah, it's an accounting conference. That's gonna be so fun [not]. Actually, that's where I came to one of Will's first talks.

Well, I was sitting in that audience. Bear in mind that I was – you know – the typical practice owner, although I wasn't completely traditional. And I was hearing these talks, and my mind completely shifted to, "we don't need this to be compliant, we need to change our whole business model!" At that point I thought, "oh my God, we're so behind!" I was like, "what are we doing? This is tech that I've never even heard of. And all of these people here, surely they're all using it!"

As it happened, they just made the change in time for the first lockdown.

"And even now I get clients from other firms come to us, and they'll say, Oh, no, I don't want to use digital tools. I want to send paperwork in. I want to basically work in the old way. An old accountant said to me that MTD is not happening, so all of this is just unnecessary stuff that you guys are introducing. Well, at that point, we've made a conscious decision to say, if you don't work this way we're not going to work with you. That was very difficult for my dad to stomach, because, turning away a client was not something that he ever did. Ever. Anyone could come and he said yes, we can do it for you. But it built something where he was working in the office seven days a week for 14 years.

That's not a life! I think this is something that he's only kind of caught on to now, because I've asked him to step in a little bit more to help whilst I'm not there with decision making and things like that because of maternity leave. And now he is using his phone to direct things. It has got teams, and he has his laptop at home, and it opened his mind. He's like, "how was I living all those years? Well I wasn't! I was just working all day long for what?" Working hard, but not smart, you know? Actually now he's coming round to what I've said to him. I know he wants to help his clients with their businesses, but actually along the way you've forgotten that you also have a business, and you also have a life. You know? You need to respect yourself first, in order for your clients to really respect you. And if the client doesn't want to work in this way, say thanks so much. See you later. Because somebody else will come along who is happy to do that.

That's what we're doing at the moment, recycling our clients. I'm not looking to grow right now. What I'm doing is where we get an enquiry from a client who is the perfect fit for us, I will look at our current client base, and see who actually we do not want to work with, who is not really doing what we want, and they're probably not paying us on time either. Then I increase their fees, or tell them, "you know we've tried. It's not working. You're better off finding somebody else." So I'll replace one with maybe three, four or five clients, both fee wise and in terms of working. And our team are happier because they're not having to chase these people non-stop.

Some clients were paying us monthly less than a phone bill, so I did a blanket fee increase, sent them an email three months before. For some it may have been triple or quadruple what they were paying. Some may have not had too much of a change. My view is that if they leave they leave, and those that stay will stay, and we will be covered from the increase in fee anyway.

For us it's a win-win essentially, and we've had some leaves out of 200 of those clients. Ten. We had ten leave.

For us as a family it has made a huge difference in getting our life back. I'm not trying to take on too much or too many other kind of businesses, anyway, because I really want to cherry pick. You know those who I really want to work with, who we can provide them the service that they need. And if we're not there yet I don't want to take them on, promise the world, and not give them what we've promised, you know? Especially with our team changing, we've lost a lot of knowledge over the years with people in our team leaving, so we're replacing that."

The pragmatic mindset –
Conversation with Chris Downing,
Director for Accountants and Bookkeepers at Sage

I asked Chris what he thought the next five to ten years would bring, and his answer was very pragmatic

"Now the trouble is because the accountant is able to actually provide that advice and guidance in the moment, it would be so easy to provide it and not get paid.

One of the biggest challenges that face accountants is to have the best quality information, great access to information inside and outside the business, but with client demands so high that they will be requesting guidance in the moment. I think that is where education is needed. Ensuring your clients see the value of what you're bringing, even though the software is surfacing a lot of information. How does the accountant fit into that journey? Not just the compliance but explaining and sharing their knowledge as well.

We will also be seeing more and more business owners seeking out an agent, an accountant, or bookkeeper. We saw that with MTD and VAT. People being concerned about working closer with HMRC. So even though the software will enable people to fill in their own items, they'll naturally be thinking, "am I paying or sending the right information to

HMRC?" The issue is that the number of accountants and bookkeepers in the UK is probably not growing [sufficiently] to meet the demand of all the new businesses. So I see a pinch point. Even though the technology will be enabling a better way of doing the data processing, there will still be huge challenges in terms of how the accountants can meet the demands of their clients. Not least because compliance has now grown fourfold in terms of quarterly reporting, even though that could be a simple business update.

Accountants will probably extend their services. Will they need specialisms in VAT, in terms of ecommerce? Because these things could be outside their normal domain, so we will probably see even more collaboration between accountants, other accountants and experts. They may extend that human element of their expertise, but also may buy in the expertise from other accountants."

Still a great opportunity

You've already read about the numbers. You know there is still a great opportunity out there and you know the reason is that cloud take-up is still pretty low. In certain regions of the UK there were only one or two firms who got it five years ago. While some are way ahead now, there's still a big gap between the front runners who understand that change is necessary and the rest of the pack.

This may be challenged by some accountants. They might say, "actually, we don't want to change. We are engaged to produce a set of accounts and do the tax". That's their mindset, not mine. It's something that we'll revisit in other chapters, as we need to think about and understand our purpose to thrive.

Most accountants I have talked to do what they do because fundamentally they want to help their clients, and they want to do this beyond just producing a set of accounts or tax return. But they can't work out how, or where to find the time to do that stuff. They see themselves as so busy doing the accounts and the tax returns and the VAT returns that there's little time left.

The starting point is the recognition that you want to be in that place, where you accept that you have a responsibility to support your clients to run better, more efficient, more profitable businesses. Businesses often ask themselves about why they are in business and we, as accountants, want to help them. So why don't accountants ask themselves that same question? Or if they do, why don't they ask it of themselves regularly enough?

I've said it before. I'll say it again. When I mentor other accounting firms, they'll get me in because they think they want to talk about technology and process. Then – without fail – we end up talking about purpose, vision, values, and pricing. These are the sticking points and the things accountants generally don't do well.

Practice doesn't make perfect

If you ask clients what they want and respond to it, you're likely building an accounting business. If you don't ask clients what they want because you think you know, you have an accounting practice.

If we treat our firm like a practice and not like a business, we don't think like a business owner thinks. Instead we think like somebody who used to have a job in an accounting firm doing accounts and tax, who now has a job in their own firm doing accounts and tax, while probably working harder and earning less.

This is bad.

That might be harsh, but it's the easiest way to demonstrate the importance of mindset. If I was writing back in 2018, I would have been quite tongue in cheek, but it's several years later. It's not my normal style to do so, but I'm genuinely concerned that you – yes you, accountants and firms – are seeing the future drift away or be stolen from you. And you're doing nothing. We're at a point where I really must be direct.

The whole point of running an accounting business is thinking "how do I build something that can operate without me?", "how can we use our trusted position to truly deliver what our clients want and need?" and "what changes and drivers for my firm can I implement that will benefit my clients too?"

"We can see we will come to the point where simply managing compliance and the client's tax position is not enough" ~ Will Farnell Digital Firm. Yes, I'm quoting myself. You see what I said there? I still want to make sure you don't miss those opportunities. Compliance is our bread and butter, but it will become more automated, get smaller and may disappear. How many times need I say it? This is why you'll see repetition. It's why I might express myself with sledgehammer force though I'd rather still be chatting to you, tongue in cheek.

Thinking allowed

I guess many people still see they're running OK businesses, making OK livings and for them the pain of changing for something better is not compelling enough. While MTD did not catalyse the change I expected and eventually became a non-event, it did stimulate a few firms to think about doing things differently. Other competitive forces are building.

Five years ago we were looking at so many low cost providers coming into the market that I thought they would start to drive accountancy companies to seek new clients higher up the food chain. Now it looks like the shift will be due to providers of the technology. Some of these providers have huge budgets and the kind of advertising that says 'hey! You don't need an accountant any more!' Irrespective of the truth, they are entering the market, here to stay and it looks likely that they'll drive out any low cost providers not established on the scene (remember Porter? – there can't be many at the low-cost low-margin end of the scale). Sole practitioners, currently looking after sole traders and smaller clients will lose them because those clients will have filed through tech companies' software. That means those smaller firms will have to start working to attract limited companies to their books. So then, the slightly bigger firms become even less interested in sole traders and more focused on limited companies. The loss of low cost competition will have a knock on effect, and each accounting firm in its turn will be forced to look for slightly bigger clients.

The digital null barrier

We discovered that migrating – or transitioning – clients to fully digital wasn't as difficult as it was presented, when we did it ourselves. Like most firms, clients trust us as advisors. This is a big perceived barrier for firms. I don't get it. Their clients will trust them and take their advice in 95 per cent of cases, so they shouldn't be using the challenge of transitioning as an excuse. Where is the recognition that we are the advisors, and that people pay us because they want us to tell them what they should do? There are accountants who don't comprehend that. It's very odd.

Change, choice and catalysis

Coming back to Covid, firms and people made the change because they had no choice. They were told they couldn't have people in their offices so they had to set them up to work at home. Before this they probably thought there was no reason to change. By the time they are losing clients on a weekly basis and the desire to change is ignited, it will probably be too late.

THE **HUMAN FIRM** by WILL FARNELL

It's really frustrating that most firms need a catalyst. So what might eventually incentivise change? Eventually, inevitably, the commoditisation of basic compliance services will drive down prices right across the sector. That is clear, but most firms have no sense of urgency. For those who already accept we have got to look at things we can do over and above compliance, they know it takes time.

Will to learn – missing the digital firm game changer

Did you miss the game changer? If you're moving your clients from Sage50 to Sage Business cloud, and think that's your cloud Accounting box ticked, you're wrong. You've done what we did in 2009. We did it then, because it was all we could do. AutoEntry didn't exist. Dext didn't exist. As soon as they existed we made the jump.

Back in 2011, that was the penny drop moment. Looking back, it was when I got over that initial thing of, "hang on a second, you don't need all the documents posted in an envelope for people to post into the system". I realised there is no envelope anymore, you could automate everything from an app on a client's phone.

This changed the whole game. It meant we could do daily or weekly bookkeeping without having to stay in a client's office. So the fundamentals, the very basic minimum that starts you off on cloud accounting was having a cloud GL and an integrated pre-accounting tool to enable your clients to record the receipts, because that way you didn't have to do the data entry. Then with the bank feed connected to drive in the bank data we had the beginnings of automation that would help us fulfil our purpose.

Process is king, data the kingdom

I've mentioned before that, in removing the element of choice, Covid proved that, as accountants and bookkeepers we all have the ability to change. The interesting thing is that we're beginning to see that the working patterns established during Covid only remain in some firms.

And that's the key. We have to be using redesigned working processes to get the real value. These processes aren't just about saving time, or helping our staff members work from home, whether in lockdown or not. The processes need to be able to provide us with an ability to deliver value. There is no point in using cloud accounting with bank feeds and only reconciling once a year, or even once a quarter! If we have the opportunity to get the bank data every day, we have the opportunity to turn it into information on a daily basis. To use that to produce information once a quarter or once a year is missing the point. So the fundamental, the very basic minimum of doing cloud accounting is having an integrated pre-accounting tool that enables your clients to use an app so that you don't have to do data entry.

Since we want to be able to talk to our client all year round and have valuable interactions, we need up to date data. This enables us to use data to help them while looking both inwards and outwards, and to identify other services we could deliver. This is only possibly by delivering existing services more efficiently, which in turn is only possible once we control the data.

Will to learn – showing who we are with App Advisory Plus

How do we, in our marketing proposition, continuously demonstrate our credibility?

Some of the answer is in that old question about whether you should be niche or generalist. Whilst I run a generalist firm, if we operated in niches it would be easier to demonstrate our knowledge. We could simply generate app stacks relevant to a particular sector and share the fact. We could build landing pages where we could demonstrate our use of tech and how it impacts the profitability of business owners. They might demonstrate the need for fewer staff, for tech automation of particular areas.

While we are generalists, we are still fussy. We'd much rather have a client that recognises the value of tech rather than one that doesn't. We hope that a client with our target profile sees our website and recognises that we can help them use their tech in their business, and that becomes part of their choice.

I recently read a LinkedIn post from a business owner who showed he was exactly the type of client we want. Almost criticising the traditional accountant's business model, he said that all his clients pay him a monthly retainer for his services and that he uses tech to make sure they get the service that they want. He asked the world why he couldn't find an accounting firm to do the same.

We want to make it clear that Farnell Clarke is a business. Not a practice or an old-style firm, but a business. And that because we run our organisation like a business we can use that experience, knowledge and perspective to help our clients.

Service above the machine learning line

And again it comes back to the accounting practice mindset, because those that are accounting businesses will see the value proposition of making the changes, and the longer term benefit, because they are thinking like business owners rather than thinking like practitioners.

It's where human input comes in. There are two aspects to considering how to gain efficiencies in accounting and tax, and both require human expertise to get it right.

Getting a tax code is fairly logical, so machines should be able to do it. Since machine learning and AI are getting better, firms' focus should be on using the machines or the AI to deal with the mundane, to enable us as the humans to do the much higher value stuff, that requires our input and experience, expertise and knowledge, and understanding of different businesses and how they work, and taking learnings from one sector and applying them to another. These are all much harder for machines.

This thinking is almost a counterbalance to the low-cost low-margin compliance-only approach. It looks at what we can do as professionals that the tech companies will never be able to. Even with AI you are never going to be able to provide that human insight and empathy and communications and all the other things that go with it.

That extends our thinking and skillsets. We need to consider how we make sure we acquire that knowledge. So when we get into thinking about what the new skillset is, we need to make sure that we are engaging with businesses in a different way to make sure that we understand what they do that works, and what doesn't, so we can learn how to take that from one sector and apply it to another...

This takes us back to other things you'll hear me talk about again and again. The idea that everyone needs to understand what the organisation is along with its purpose, that the client experience is key and the wonderful idea of gross recurring fees, all of which you will read about elsewhere in this book.

Will to learn – our biggest backtrack

Five years ago we used only Xero and imposed that on our clients, explaining why. We don't do this exclusively now, and it's the most significant service based change – and change in emphasis - that we've made. As we have grown we have become able to create dedicated teams (pods) that are able to support particular software solutions. This has enabled us to broaden our offer and not dilute our efficiency.

In the past, had a potential client come to us wanting to use Sage instead of Xero, we would have suggested that they find a firm somewhere else. It's always important to make sure that our client understands the value to them of what we suggest that they do, and we knew we would serve our clients more efficiently by sticking to a single platform. I would still suggest that smaller practices start by picking a system and then stick to it for the same reason.

The shift in our thinking has come partly because of scaling up and partly through redesigning our processes to be broader in what we offer to our clients whilst spreading the risk of being dependent on a single supplier. While it still serves our client-centric purpose, it's the biggest backtrack of what I said in the previous book.

The take-home

Think about what you want the new firm to be

- Change your mindset, think like a business to survive and thrive,
- Getting it wrong fast, and learning is important,
- There's still opportunity.

Notes

PART TWO

MAKING
IT GROW

Growing your firm is easy. Scaling it less so. The challenge comes
as we grow, being able to consistently deliver on the things that
we say and tell clients that we're going to do. This section looks at
how to achieve seamless scalability, bring staff and clients along
with you, suggests ways to approach the thinking behind change,
transitioning and structuring to a scalable organisation, and the
consequences if you are not willing and ready to change.

It's easy to grow, hard to scale
and the thinking never stops

7

Scalability, Staff and Super-Evolution

THEN

"The more automated your processes are, then the more scalable your business will be."

NOW

"Scaling requires a constant state of rethinking."

Growing is easy. Scaling is different. The challenge comes as we grow, being able to consistently deliver on the things that we say and tell the client that we're going to deliver for them.

We need to plan for scale – Farnell Clarke has. There is consistency of timing as to when firm owners hit hurdles. Give or take about 10 per cent, that happens at eight people, 15 people, 23 people, 35 people, 50 people and as we've seen at Farnell Clarke recently, 70 people has its challenges. Going on from that, I've also spoken to accounting firm owners who have grown further and they have already prepared me for the challenges we're likely to meet at 100 people

It's really fascinating. In a recent call discussing scaling, I mentioned it to another guy who said they had real hurdles at that magic number eight. He found himself working in the business, not on the business. He's at nine people, so the challenges make sense size-wise.

Scalability is the ability of a business to seamlessly grow and to handle an increasing amount of work on demand whilst maintaining or improving its quality, service, efficiency and profitability without detriment to the client experience or the firm. In the human firm this is essential to serve an expanding client base.

To achieve scalability, an organisation must design its infrastructure to accommodate and anticipate growth. This includes creating efficient, repeatable and scalable processes and procedures, investing in the automation of any remaining routine tasks and ensuring that employees are sufficiently skilled to handle the workloads. Done properly this means firms will be able to serve their clients better by maintaining excellent communications, providing great quality timely responses to queries, (through excellent quality up-to-the-minute data), and well considered insights and services.

Processes and procedures must be both clear and easily replicable. Standardised workflows, checklists and templates are vital, and consistent use across the firm means that clients receive a consistent level of service regardless of the size of the firm or the number of clients being served. The challenge to this is that things drift as they grow – it created challenges for us at Farnell Clarke – and as firm owner we get further away from what's happening on a day-to-day basis. Understanding this, and managing it so that pods work consistently throughout the firm, without developing idiosyncratic approaches, politics or processes is one of the things we need to guard against, from the start. I call it silo creep, where people get into the habit of doing things slightly differently. We have learned of the need to continually check and capture that which, as the compound effect of those little tweaks to process can lead to significant change, if left unchallenged.

Single process good, multiple processes bad – Conversation with James Kay, Managing Director, Farnell Clarke

I wanted to get James' take on achieving scalability, infrastructure design to accommodate and anticipate growth, the creation of efficient repeatable and scalable processes and procedures and automation. And whether you agree that done properly this means that firms can serve their clients better both through excellent up-to-the-minute data, great communications and well considered insights and services. Here's the answer, in his words;

"Let's start with the processes. Repeatable, scalable processes. It has always been about working with the minimal number of processes, and the minimal number of products required to do the process. And of course working with the best of breed for those products.

The point of that is, a lot of firms work with different sorts of software and multiple processes, and that is very much client-led. The client says they want an accountant to do something, and they do it. Which of course means more staff training, and more processes, which inevitably leads to inefficiency.

So we've always put in place single processes wherever possible. That means it's easy to train, and easier for staff to learn and support each other and know what is going on. The purpose for us is that with the fixed price model we benefit from those efficiencies, while if you are charging for your time, the client end up paying for your firm's inefficiencies."

So, single fixed processes are good because the client benefits from our efficiencies, and multiple processes are bad, because the client pays for our inefficiencies.

Here's James again;

"So obviously the single process then makes it much easier to predict what resource a new client coming in would need. So we can look to scalability. We can look at a client and say right, we know that the resources needed for that client are X and Y. And hopefully, we can plan for our growth much more easily because of that certainty around the service that we offer, and the processes that we have in place. We are a growing business so we always aim to have capacity."

And that in itself, is a challenge.

"In this industry the people are the most difficult aspect of scaling. We always try to recruit ahead of new work coming in. We don't like to take any work on, and not be ready for it. Whether that new work means that a client needs a whole person to themselves, or that we need to make sure we have capacity for a team to take on several new clients."

Then there is scope creep...

"Managing scope creep is difficult. Since the last book we are far better at identifying where we are. We've really had to push a much more commercial mindset down to the teams. That has involved giving them more access to their own financial performance. We've given the client managers more responsibility over the fees that the clients are paying. And certainly have more visibility of that all the way through the team, and ultimately responsibility to make sure that their team is profitable."

Balloons and scaling –
Conversation with James Ashford, VP of GoProposal by Sage

In one of our many conversations about growth and scaling, James said this;

"I always like to visualise things. So I picture 'growth' to be like inflating a balloon. It gets bigger, but the amount of substance doesn't increase; it's

Growth, Scaling and Stagnating

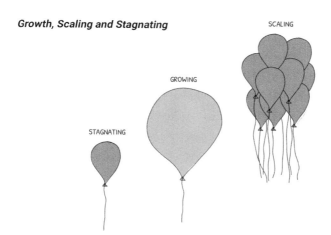

just because it's stretched and more vulnerable to being burst. Scaling is when you've got the balloon blown to a reasonable size, and then you add more balloons. And the more you add, the higher they will take you, safely."

The scale struggle

So why do firms struggle to scale? Firstly, it's not their fault. They are trained in how to be an expert in their craft, but not in how to scale a successful, profitable, accounting business, in a post Covid, post digitised world. I think many aspects of how the business needs to run sits in the heads of a few people, rather than baked into predictable systems, that enable the entire team to operate optimally.

A scalable firm should run on systems and then the people should run the systems. Too many firms are run by people. People then think that if a firm is run on systems and processes and uses high levels of automation, that dehumanises the firm. Well, the absolute opposite is true. If you can remove as much of the unnecessary thinking and worry and heavy lifting as possible, you actually free up your team to be their creative, human, best selves. They become free to have real, human interaction and deliver the greatest impact they can. It's then about getting out of their way and creating a culture that allows them to flourish, to take risks, experiment and drive your business forward.

You – the owner, partner or founder – can't actually scale your business, all you can do is put in the foundations that support scalability, and then grow and develop your team. They in turn will scale the business.

> **Super-evolution**
> Super-evolution is the fast and seamless scaled growth of an organisation through consistent change based on fulfilling the organisation's purpose.

To 100 and beyond

In talking to me about his firm, Acuity, Kenji Kuramoto talked about the challenges scaling up to 150 staff members in 18 years. He said just by the fact they serve fast growing entrepreneurial software companies they are immersed in tech, which meant they were happy to see and take on accountancy-related innovation as it happened and excited when larger ERP systems started moving to the cloud. Whilst scaling up they stayed human within the firm and with their clients. "There was not a single entrepreneur that said, "Oh, I can't wait to do my own accounting and do my own financial work," as part of becoming an entrepreneur. So we wanted to step in and fill that gap and help them." Meanwhile he talked about the importance of getting and keeping the right people, and how they gave him a lightbulb moment of why he gets most clarity about how much – and how quickly – the firm can scale. He went on to share both mistakes and key learning points as he and his partner figured out how to scale up to meet a high supply-and-demand curve that is still growing today.

The take-home

The keys to seamless scalability, and the success of bringing staff – and through staff, to clients – as long as an organisation scales include:

- Transparency through great communications and clear career planning,
- Giving them the training, support, tech and processes they require,
- Empowering them fully.

Scale up with pod structures
and by recognising what
others do better

8

Scalability and the De-Willing Progression

THEN

"De-Willing was the first significant step to facilitate growth."

NOW

"Internal team creation and pod structures have proven the best enabler for scaling."

In the Digital Firm I wrote that de-Willing was Frances' and James' shorthand for the way I took a step back from day-to-day operations to concentrate on strategy, business development and business alliances. We've grown now, and new directors have taken on very specific roles.

Growth – and the scaling required – now requires a constant state of rethinking. Building our leadership team to enable our business to go to the next level is a constant challenge. The principal of de-Willing is the same, and while you could say we're de-Francesing and de-Jamesing, it's more about growth and building the leadership team to put us in a position to be able to continue scaling. Ultimately, we have a choice: build a valuable resilient firm, or stay the undisputed bosses of something that will always be smaller.

"

> *Ultimately we have a choice: build a valuable resilient firm, or stay the undisputed bosses of something that will always be smaller.*

"

In terms of thinking about the ability for firms to scale, the structure has got to be right. The business owner or partners or principals will block the growth if they hang on to all the client relationships. We knew this, so thought about how to build a structure that gives us – and our quality control – confidence that client relationships could be managed effectively. The traditional top-down approach also tends to have decision-making centralised among a few individuals, none of whom have very much time. This can lead to stagnation, partly because there's so little time for strategic planning and partly because new ideas are hamstrung by the need to get sign-off from those already-too-busy people in charge.

Will to learn – a constant state of rethinking

As we grew, we evolved our company structure with this in mind. Originally we allocated our clients' somebody who managed personal tax, someone in accounts, someone else responsible for payroll and somebody else for VAT and bookkeeping. We tried a number of different structures, and our clients just got confused. They told us so! They'd say "I used to talk to Will but can't talk to him any more and I don't know who to call".

So we revisited the model and decided to give each client someone who we called an account handler; the client's first point of contact. We allocated the role to junior staff members and they just weren't up to the job. They weren't experienced enough to answer a lot of the clients' questions straight off, and often weren't confident of which client-supporting action to prioritise. That lack of experience meant they didn't know what they needed to work on first.

Rather than confused, our clients became frustrated. So, we decided to have another good think about how to manage the situation. We decided to recruit more senior client managers and gave them the support they needed to manage the client relationships.

That became the start of our pod structures, (a great way to plan scalability for future growth because they help you think ahead to where business is coming from and from that identify gaps and therefore the type of staff you need to recruit). While we have evolved the pods themselves, we find they really, really work. At the start we thought that a pod would comprise a team of four people, and that team could deliver us about £250,000 revenue. It almost didn't matter what the client mix was. One pod might have 50 clients and another might have 100 clients, but they could all deliver £250,000 of revenue based on the structure that we created. At the time of writing this book, that £250,000 had risen to £300,000 due partially to inflation and partially to our regular prices revisit.

Pods and smaller firms

What we've seen is that irrespective of the size of a firm, pod structures help. For smaller firms the owner will sit in the client manager role while assessing whether a second pod is needed as part of that growth with the business owner continuing to operate a pod, or does the business owner want to step out of day-to-day work to continue to drive the business. As part of that, the business can continue to think about potential gaps and how they might be filled with tech, process and recruitment.

Here are some basic pod structure questions for smaller firms

- Do I want to stay as both firm owner and client manager?
- When we grow do I want to create a second pod?
- Where are the gaps in terms of skills and recruitment?
- Do we need a trainee at the bottom or a senior who is really comfortable creating a set of accounts that I as business owner can review in the client manager role?
- Do I have a senior who is about ready to step up to client manager role?
- What is the capacity limit above which I need another pod?

The Farnell Clarke Pod Structure

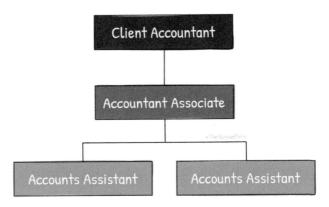

It's worth mentioning that within this pod structure we would have a couple of apprentice-type trainees. Now, our pod structure is about making sure that that we build the right team to support the client in the right way to deliver the right client touchpoints. Because the pods in our firm deliver almost everything that a client needs with the exception of payroll, (which is run centrally), and can access wider services within the firm through the client manager, we have eliminated the client's confusion of who they should talk to. Our clients don't necessary know them as 'pods'. To them, a pod is simply their accounts team, and they know if they can't get hold of one person someone else will be around.

From a gross profit point of view it gave us real clarity over what the team could deliver. We know the revenue, the cost base and a simple calculation enables us to understand the contribution to the firm along with the point at which the pod gets full, (over £300,000 and we can't expect more). That gives us the clarity to plan and create a new pod. And if you are delivering consistent double digit growth – as we are – there will always be opportunities for people to step up within the firm by moving into a new pod.

Will to learn – make mistakes quickly and learn from them

If I had my time again, I would have let go of many of the things I had clung on to. In 2016 we had got to the point of being almost a million pound revenue business and I was still doing things like opening the post! I had recognised that I needed to step back from some of the things that I had clung on to, but letting go was another matter. Clearly if I wanted to scale I had to recognise the things that only I could do, and let go of all the things that other people could do, and in many cases do better than me.

In the Digital Firm, I talked about the early stuff, about me allowing other people to take control of the things that I wasn't great at to enable me to focus on the things I was good at. That set the scene. But it's important to rethink the structure that you have in place to run and manage a firm whatever size you are at.

That's where we are again, and our first attempt to de-Frances and de-James proved really difficult. It has meant that the three of us have had to refocus, to step back into some of the things that we had hoped to let go of. As Frances Kay says, "make mistakes quickly and learn from them". We've learned from our mistakes and can see now that actually we weren't ready to leave aspects of our roles completely. We now know that's because we didn't have the right structure and the right people in place.

From principals to principles

"

> *As we grew, things changed, the one constant being that scaling requires a constant state of rethinking.*

"

In fact, the pod structure enables us to fluidly create that flow of new client managers and new seniors from our pool of trainees. They can see how they might progress. And meanwhile, the pod structure became a really flexible way for us to manage clients, to have client managers managing those client relationships, to scale, and ultimately by having client managers managing those client relationships the firm principals are not tied to client relationships so can spend time thinking about growing the business, strategy and all the other things that will enable them to deliver on their own objectives.

Once we got the client management structure right, we were able to think about other things that could be done to build the firm's leadership team. Just as de-Willing was an essential step in the scaling process, the creation of pod structures was another because they facilitated growth through scaling and freed up management time. We needed it. As we grew things changed, the one constant being that scaling requires a constant state of rethinking. Along with this came the will to undertake more de-Willing and empower the management team.

Eventually we brought in Tim Youngman, a stand-alone director tasked with driving our marketing activity and meeting strategic growth objectives. Then Lauren Sanders joined us, as HR Director who faces both inwards and outwards. Ultimately there was little or no De-Jamesing or De-Francesing because change had become more about building the leadership team to enable the business to reach its next level.

More on why pods are useful

- They enable collaboration and communication across areas of expertise and the firm,

- They are more agile, nimble and adaptable which means they can respond to clients quickly,

- They make it easier to work cross-functionally, allowing people with complementary skill sets to work together meaning fewer bottlenecks,

- We can better cater to our clients, as pods allow better alignment with each client, better client touchpoints, and a closer relationship allowing a full understanding of the client's personal and business needs, priorities, values and goals,

- They instil a sense of accountability and traceability since pods are accountable for the client from start to finish,

- They allow a streamlining of workflows by breaking down silos, increasing communication and collaboration,

- Then allow us to service clients with different app stacks, since each pod can specialise,

- Breaking down traditional silos is key to surviving and thriving in our customer-centric world. The pod model – a way of working that is based around small teams of people with complementary skills – is the ideal way to overcome these silos and scale quickly. It offers employees flexible autonomous working arrangements, helps streamline workflows, ensures alignment with client goals and needs, provides sensible touchpoints and helps staff members understand how and where their careers can progress and allows the business to scale.

How to transition

Making the switch can seem daunting, but careful planning and execution with careful attention to your cloud-based processes will help.

1. **Start with a single pod.** Using it as a project to test ideas and make adjustments before rolling it out firm-wide. Go from a theoretical process to a test case on a small appropriate client, then when everyone is comfortable grow it.

2. **Keep partners or principals out.** Of course you need executive support, but if they are part of the pod you're not actually improving the system. Give pod teams their head.

3. **Create clearly defined roles within each pod and keep everything transparent, repeatable and sustainable.** If you are going with clients with different app stacks (we scaled into it) use different pods for each.

4. **Don't make the pod too big or too small.** They need to have a mix of skill sets but not be unwieldy.

5. **Encourage cross-pod communication.** Each pod should learn from others and share information and insights. This needs horizontal communication channels of course.

6. **Give yourself time.** It takes significant time and resources to get the pod structure right for your firm, your clients and your staff. Accept this and get feedback from each pod iteration to improve things.

7. **Be explicit in how the pod structure facilitates staff members' career development.** Relate this to the firms vision and values so everyone knows where they fit.

8. **Don't stop talking.** Just because you're not at the client-facing coalface doesn't mean you're not needed. Vision and values, purpose and passion are firm-wide characteristics that need active maintenance.

9. **Be open.** De-Will (or de-whoever) your principals in the pod creation process, this should be iterative and something your management team should always bear in mind.

The take-home

- A pod based organisation is easily scalable, easily understood in terms of gross profit, and enables internal staff development,

- It also frees the firms principals to think more strategically and deliver on their own objectives,

- If your principals stay the main point of contact for your clients – in any structure – they'll stay the undisputed bosses of something that is smaller and less resilient. Our solution is pod structures.

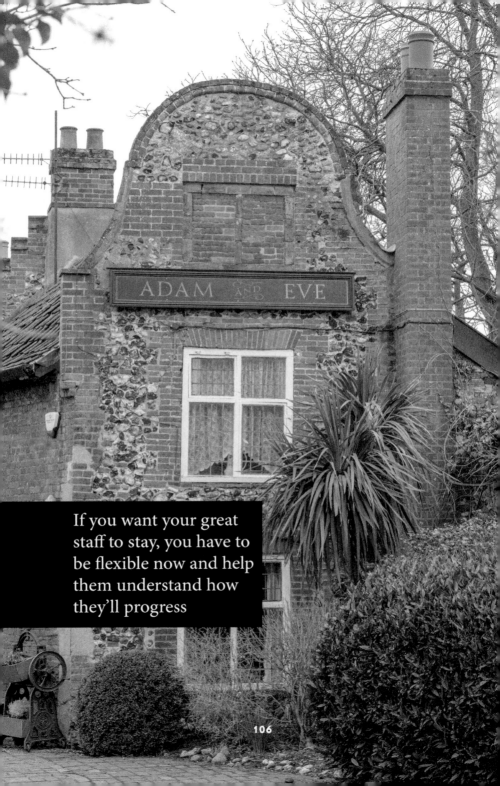

If you want your great staff to stay, you have to be flexible now and help them understand how they'll progress

9

Staff and Scalability

THEN

"Getting the right staff in the right place with the right training at the right time is vital to your future success. They need to want to stay with your firm and be engaged with and add value to your clients."

NOW

"It's not enough that there are opportunities for progression, or that people can see the firm grow. To make people want to stay you need to be explicit, outline career pathways and demonstrate progression."

As you've read, I believe that growing your firm is quite easy. Scaling an accounting firm is much harder. It means working harder, living by its values, an openness to change and a lot more. Conventional accounting firms have to keep bringing partners on. While some firms manage to grow this way, it is potentially unsustainable. For us, the fact that as principals we don't hold direct client relationships gives us a greater ability to scale.

We're in a growing market. One of the challenges of recruiting is that the people you recruit need to deliver growth. Whereas the rigid hierarchy of a partnership model becomes unwieldy, and works only with indefinite recruitment or promotion of new partners to service new clients, our pod structure makes our business scalable, firstly – as you know – because we're delegating client 'ownership' and secondly to provide our clients with speedy access to the expertise they need.

Make the most of this recruitment from a marketing point of view, for clients as well as for new joiners. The thing many firms often miss is that they don't treat recruitment as a marketing activity. To avoid this lost opportunity, when you're marketing for talent you need to get across the flexibility you offer along with the values that underpin your firm's purpose, so that both potential team members and clients looking for an accounting firm that aligns to their values can clearly see that you do.

Yes, there is more flexibility now than there was pre-Covid – particularly in the world of accounting – but the likelihood is that many firms are still very much office based, which makes those firms offering some level of flexibility more attractive in the world we operate in now.

As I said early on, accountants are not generally good at adapting. While it seems bonkers to me, it often takes regulation or a significant event to catalyse significant change.

Covid and job flexibility

While many forward-thinking businesses – including accountants and bookkeepers – were prepared to offer workplace flexibility pre-Covid, the pandemic has increased the expectation of staff that flexibility in both hours and location be given.

Farnell Clarke had already moved from a nine-to-five mentality to 'do the job how you want as long as it gets done properly'. That gave us a unique advantage in terms of recruitment, because we were offering flexibility when the majority of other firms were not. Don't get me wrong, despite increasing flexibility for staff that has come as a result of Covid, most accounting firms are still office based. They expect their teams to be in the office five days a week. They might not even have a choice, since flexibility is conferred by use of the right tech, and those using tech throughout the entire firm, are still in the minority.

It makes sense to create an internal structure within which people can recognise how they can be promoted and grow. Whilst we created pods at Farnell Clarke to serve the client better, we were careful in their design, ensuring that the pod structure serves our employees too.

"

> *It is our responsibility to make sure that our teams understand where we are going, and that there are clearly defined paths in terms of promotion and career development opportunities.*

"

For me, there is no better way of growing a team than internally. At Farnell Clarke we create jobs so that people can move around and be promoted effectively. And while we created the pods partly to serve the client better, they have also been created so that people can see their potential career pathways within the firm. So bringing people in, training them in the way that we want them to work and ensuring that they recognise the business is growing and opportunities are created all the time is one of the things we sorted years ago.

I discovered that Eriona Bajrakurtaj has an interesting perspective on staff training and the balance of flexibility and working from the office in a recent conversation;

"Coming out of Covid, we did ask the team to come back a few days in the office, and a few days from home, because I do think fully working from home is not ideal. You don't get that culture or camaraderie or – you know – training. Or if you need to ask something quickly, when you're in the office, and say someone has a query, you will overhear what their issue is and how they resolved it.

What we try to do is every two weeks we would have the team kind of send messages to one person say, "I'd like an update on this" or "I'm not sure how to do that." We put a list together, and every two weeks we go through that list. Without saying who asked for it, we present it as a refresher, so that everybody gets that training.

But I don't think it's as effective as being in the office. Hence why, I think we're never going to be fully working from home. We are always going to be a mix, also for the relationship with the team. We connect with each other via teams, and we try to be as friendly and so on as possible, but again, it's not the same as meeting up with each other."

Will to learn – communicating consistently

Very early on back in 2015 we lost six staff in eight weeks. About 20 per cent of our workforce at the time, it was quite a blow. The key message in our exit interviews was that the people who left couldn't see opportunities for them to develop in the firm. It was a big awakening for me because at the time we were growing at 40 per cent a year. I thought "what do you mean you can't see the opportunities? You can see that we're bringing in new clients, that we've moved offices, and that we're growing as a business, so what do you mean you can't see the opportunities?" The key point – which until then I had not done consistently but that we now know we must do – is to make sure that everyone in our teams understand where we are going, and that they can see clearly defined paths in terms of promotion and career development opportunities.

From competency framework to client experience

On the back of that we started to build our competency frameworks, our pay bandings and all the things that let people say "well... if I do X, Y and Z I then get promoted to this grade, and this is what it means in terms of values and responsibilities and this is what I'm going to get paid."

Lauren Sanders, our HR Director, explains further;

"We rolled up our competency framework in April last year, which precedes me slightly. Having seen it bed in to our appraisal process, to our one-to-ones, just integrating it into development, it was actually very much a starting point. What we're finding now is that it should be different for different departments, for example tax. It's not necessarily a one-size-fits all approach.

For me, a competency framework should never be rolled out as a finished article. We need to continually assess and reassess it. That is one of my priorities for our next quarter, use it to find out what the skill sets we have within the company, what we need and identify the gaps and opportunities. If we can use the competency framework effectively, it's not just a paper exercise. It helps us identify where we've got our high performance people and then look at how that fits in the succession, planning. We can use it to identify knowledge experts and plan better knowledge management.

We need a competency framework and one that clearly states the expectations that we have, the things we want, and the things we need. So it filters into so many different aspects of the people journey from recruitment to development, and helps us reward performance as well. It's critical to one roll out, but the trick is to never see it as a finished article. It evolves. It's kind of your Ground Zero of people management."

So, the key message here is that we can't assume these things. We have to be really clear. We have to engage with our people and show them what they need to do and where they need to go. The motivations and needs of more recent generations, (particularly around GenZ), are almost too new for me to be able to suggest what might best appeal to them with confidence, when we read the research and talk to them, they tell us they genuinely care. They want to understand what their contribution is, what role they are playing, how they are contributing to the organisation they've chosen to be part of, and what they can do to offer greater contribution they can make in supporting the organisation they are linked to, and they choose organisations as clients and to work with because they believe in the visions and values.

Again, if you don't have performance management frameworks and an organisational structure that enables people to understand the organisational objectives they are supporting and are linked to, and if this is not clearly related to the entire business, you're unlikely to keep the best staff. From this it's a short jump to understand that lifetime value as a business decision – about which you will read more later – takes a deeper meaning since it needs to relate both to clients and to staff. It means there should be a way to trace and link the organisation's overarching objectives and everyone's individual objectives, and a way for people to understand how that 'thing' on their personal objectives enables them to contribute to the organisation as a whole.

Glassdoor

Founded in the US, Glassdoor, by servicing the shifted priorities of recent generations, is one of the fastest growing jobs and recruiting sites. Alongside job adverts it holds a growing database of millions of company reviews, CEO approval ratings, salary reports, interview reviews and questions, benefits reviews, office photos and more.

Bringing things together

Taking this on a level, everybody needs to understand what the firm is, what it's trying to achieve, expectations for teams pods and individuals, what the ideal client experience level is and the reasons for these things. And they need to be comfortable with it. That means understanding our purpose. From there, if we think about client experience as a concept, the client experience becomes the total sum of every touchpoint you have with the client, from their first engagement with your organisation to the very last.

And finally, here's an extract from a job ad I found on LinkedIn. Written by LisaDanels of Human Edge, it is bang-on message.

> "We are dynamic and fast-growing company with a strong ambition to propel organizations forward by maximizing their human potential. Imagine if organizations could propel faster with thriving teams, people energized by tapping into their core talents and inspired by company purpose. Enabling organizations and people to thrive is core to everything we believe — core to teams, core to leadership, core to growth.
>
> To realize this, we're building a stellar team in which you will be challenged tremendously and where you will work with a high level of autonomy. Apart from having the independence to move the needle and make an impact, you'll be surrounded by an open team that is there to support you along the way.
>
> ...At Human Edge we embrace the agile mindset and strive to continuously improve the way we do things. We are passionate about what we do and work in an environment where we value innovation, creativity, and open communication. The pursuit of bringing human potential to life is at the CORE of everything we do to create value for our customers.
>
> Come as you are! We're looking for amazing people with diverse backgrounds, experiences, abilities, and perspectives. Human Edge welcomes and encourages diversity in the workplace."

and . . .

At Human Edge we are looking for talents that…

- **Commitment** – *Acts as an owner of human edge and is committed to go above and beyond to deliver to customer expectations and drive business growth,*

- **Accountability** – *Holds self accountable, following through on commitments, and taking ownership of successes and failures,*

- **Excellence** – *Takes pride in work, striving for excellence and working to establish an outstanding level of professional delivery,*

- **Results** – *Delivers against commitments by driving tasks to completion,*

- **Team** – *Works closely with others towards a common vision or goal, and actively shares responsibility and rewards, and contributes to the success of the team."*

An alternative view

Brian Coventry's diagram describes the elements required for a firm to ensure their employees are working to the best of their abilities, are rewarded for their performance and have a healthy work-life balance. Understanding the interplay between these four elements enables an accounting firm to create an environment conducive to employee success.

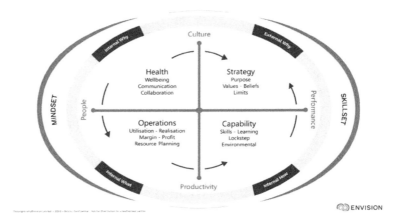

> **Will to learn – AccountantsOnline**
> I've heard that AccountantsOnline in Ireland pay for a company to constantly review competitive salaries and actively increase them in their firm across roles, sometimes with big leaps, to make sure they're retaining staff. Whether this is relevant or not, it's an interesting approach to staff retention, especially considering the firm personality that it shows.

The take-home

Ignore the work-life priorities of Millennials, and Generations Z and Alpha at your peril. Show flexibility, clear career paths, organisational structures and potential remuneration clearly or risk losing staff to those who do.

The pod structure helps staff members understand what is expected of them and can be used to demonstrate each individual's potential career progression. This is particularly important for Millennials and Gen Z people who need to understand not just what they are doing and how it helps the organisation as a whole, but also how their growing contributions matter and are rewarded and that their personal objectives and values are aligned to that of the firm.

Structure for scalability

10

Scalability, and the Human Firm

THEN

"Evolution isn't a destination, rather a continuous journey."

NOW

"Driven by tech, technologists, scientists, behaviourists and engineers the coming change will fundamentally and irrevocably transform all industries."

Super-evolution and the Human Firm

We live in an era in which the increasing pace of technology development is running parallel to radical, multigenerational change. Driven by technologists, scientists, behaviourists and engineers, the process of super-evolution will fundamentally and irrevocably transform all industries.

Increased accessibility to data, ubiquitous computing, better and more joined-up communications are going to change emerging technologies. Such tech will make it possible to do things faster, better and cheaper, and will help us as accountants come up with new insights for our clients and make radical improvements to our firms, our way of working and the way we scale. Tech development cycles that once took years can now be completed in days.

I've said it before, but it's clear that eventually the old-style partner-based firm with traditional decision-making hierarchy will not be able to keep up. Consider that many younger professional accountants are already more interested in buying houses than into a firm, particularly one achieving single digit growth. What will firms do from a succession point of view if they are not growing sufficiently fast and creating value for potential partners? Another way in which the partnership model is already potentially flawed.

The pod model reduces the friction of a traditional firm's partner-based decision making structure. It blends information and services more holistically, creating sustainable growth. It gives confidence to client and staff members for related but different reasons. It reduces the likelihood of the evolution of problems that may disrupt growth or may prevent you from scaling. It means individuals in pods who have great ideas regarding client service can pass them to other pods. It flexes when confronted with unanticipated challenges, and frees the firm's principals to consider the future and what it involves.

This is agile accounting. Agile in the truest meaning – not the much – used and less-understood development framework, but something that can scale, respond to external challenges and grow. I've already challenged you to really consider the best value for your clients. There may be other ways to respond to an uncertain future, but the pod structure works and is ours.

Casting about pods – Conversation with Stefan Barrett

I discussed the pod structure with Stefan Barrett, too;

Stefan: I like your approach of being able to have two pods, with Sage experts over here and Xero experts over here, so you can accommodate clients with both, but we can't do that. We don't have the facility to do that.

Though I see that if I was to times my team by two I could effectively have two Bee Motion conveyor belts, one for Sage and one for Xero and could link them together. But I'll probably still only stay with Sage because I know how much they're investing and know where they're going in the future. I feel that they're really upping the ante in respect to investment.

Will: I think it's similar for us. We've got to a scale where it's not harder to take people on another platform, it's just recognising what is needed. Now we're working with some bigger clients in our outsourcing team, they're beyond Xero and using almost entry-level ERP systems, so that's driving a bit of change from the model we've got. A few years ago, I spent a year on Sage's Partner Advisory Council when we were a 100 per cent Xero practice and it was fascinating. So I've seen the progress and the acquisitions. A cracking job.

The take-home

The pod structure makes a firm more resilient, now and in the foreseeable future.

Notes

PART THREE

MAKING A DIFFERENCE

**How to differentiate the firm,
why and how to measure progress.**

This section shows through numbers and discussion why those
who become fully digital are still early adopters. It discusses how
the delivery of professional services – and firm success – can be
delivered in a new and authentic way through the clear articulation
of purpose and suggests that Client Lifetime Value can be used
both as metric and motivator.

Meaningful conversation and
the conversion resistance chasm

11

In the Numbers

THEN

"That we were providing a service nobody else was, using new tech, was a key part of our growth, and at the point of publishing this book there was still an opportunity to be gained in moving quickly."

NOW

"There still is."

Farnell Clarke have always been innovators. We were so early on the early adopter curve that we often weren't able to find tech to fulfil particular business needs. Years later, I am still amazed at how slowly the sector has adopted tools that would enable both firms and their clients to be more efficient, useful and productive and join the discussion regularly. I've thought hard about why this might be, and about what is behind it. This book summarises the results.

Five years ago, in The Digital Firm, I talked about 20 per cent of adoption of cloud tech in the UK. Five years on I'm still saying it. That tells me that five years ago I was really ambitious and overestimated the level of adoption. I think that's bonkers, and it is worth considering why.

Let's assume that cloud adoption means just the adoption of a cloud-based GL, automated receipt scanning and the bank feed connected to drive in your bank data. If cloud adoption just means those few things then maybe we're into an early majority of adopters, about 20 per cent in the UK.

Full digitisation is key. If only 20 per cent of the market has moved to the cloud, that means 80 per cent of the market is still looking at data that is 18 months old! Those firms haven't felt the pain enough to make them change. Sadly external regulations like MTD aren't likely to change that any time soon.

Will to learn – trust and meaningful conversation

At Farnell Clarke, timely data from full cloud adoption and the right app stacks mean that we are able to start meaningful conversations with our clients about what else we could do to help their businesses become more efficient and ultimately profitable. Although many firms expect their clients will either be uninterested in anything beyond core compliance, and respond negatively, whenever we approach our clients, they are universally receptive to our ideas. That's because there is already an element of trust between us. It means that with the right relationship and timely data, new clients would come to us first and quickly, with every business question they have. For me this is the true essence of delivery advisory services. And we want them to! Trust is key, in the Human Firm.

That brings us back to the 20 per cent of full cloud adopters who are at an advantage, having moved to full cloud adoption and the 80 per cent who are not. My view is that we are still in the early adoption stage.

Crossing the chasm

In 1962 the sociologist Everett Rogers used the idea of The Chasm as a way of discussing different types of buyers and their resistance to innovation. He posited that each type of buyer feels more comfortable using others in their reference base, (innovators, early adopters, pragmatists, conservatives and sceptics), from their own group. In this, the Chasm represents the credibility gap since people in each group take longer to believe in references from a group to their left, and suggested segmentation as a way to get adoption between one group of people and the next.

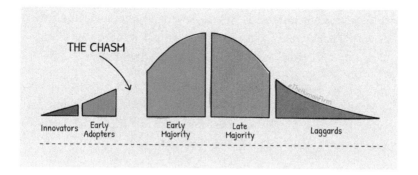

Back to my statement that only 20 per cent of people are doing cloud accounting. We know that there are a bunch of people that have and use cloud-based GLs. That means they have clients in the cloud but are not using pre-accounting tools which for me is one of the pre-requisites. There are also some with cloud licences that are not being used, others who really are digitally enabled accountants who have successfully blended people, process and technology.

Depending on who you listen to, there are between 34,000 and 70,000 accounting firms in the UK. At the lower end of this, you can see that the partner numbers for pre-accounting tools are still amazingly low. And that means the numbers of those who are using a full app stack, with pre-accounting tools, payment tools, reporting tools, well thought-through processes and other specialist tech are even lower. If I put my overambitious 2018 hat on, the likelihood is that only 20 per cent of that 20 per cent are doing it well.

The numbers

Accounting software companies indicated there were about 400,000 users of cloud accounting software in the UK in 2018. It's well over that now. The 4.5 million small UK businesses I mentioned in The Digital Firm has risen to 5.9 million today. A rough calculation – based on numbers from app providers – would have us at about 1.4 million cloud accounting subscribers. But software companies count sold licenses, and accountants often sit on thousands of these not in use.

And that is the starting point. Because if all they have done is what I mentioned above, if they have adopted a cloud GL, without pre-accounting tools, AutoEntry, Dext and Hubdoc, they can't really be considered as having adopted cloud accounting.

Let's play another thought game to put this in context. For the sake of argument I am making an assumption that Dext have roughly 10,000 partners globally with 4,000-7,000 accounting firm partners in the UK, (which bear out these back-of-a-fag-packet calculations nicely). Then I will assume that you can be a Dext partner if you've got five clients. If a firm has 100 clients and only five are using Dext, are they really a cloud accounting firm? I'd suggest that unless at least 75 per cent of eligible clients are using cloud accounting tech, they are not.

That's why I believe we are still talking early adoption. Even if we're not, we'd be at the early stage of the chasm or – very much less likely – just about touching into early majority. To bring our clients with us therefore needs clear thought, good services, and trust.

The silver lining

Without full cloud-based automation and regular, (daily or weekly) bookkeeping we don't get current data. Without current data we can't use tools like Futrli, Fathom and Spotlight to churn out valuable insights. Without such apps we can't provide really useful information to our clients. If we can't provide such services to our clients, they are ultimately likely to go to firms that can. This might seem superficially like bad news, but in fact it is not. The fact that so few firms have fully adopted cloud accounting means that huge opportunities abound.

Why is adoption so slow? –
Conversation with Chris Downing

I asked Chris Downing of Sage why he thought so few firms have fully moved to the cloud. Here's what he said.

"Are we still waiting for the technology to be even better? For example, let's take receipt capture. Yes, it may be the bedrock of any progressive firm; the ability to take paper records, transform them into data and allow it to flow into your preferred bookkeeping tool. However, though great as a practice workflow tool – AutoEntry, Dext and Hubdoc when introduced as part of the clients' tech stack alongside collaborative bookkeeping, does create unnecessary friction, training and touch points for the market majority being small business owners or sole traders. They want a single solution, an app with all the capabilities of many.

If you go back in time to Covid, there was a huge driving force towards cash flow management. We could see the chat on social media. What did they want to use? Fluidly? Float? Futrli? Fathom? People would say, "Oh, no, I just want to use an excel spreadsheet". Why? Because the business didn't even use one piece of tech, so you couldn't get the data for the others. So they were just looking at taking some bank feeds, dropping it into Excel and seeing the information. There was a huge new benefit for those custom reports, but the barrier was always the client's lack of bookkeeping tools.

The game changing tech exists, the demand exists, but still adoption is slow. I believe the other challenge to be resolved is awareness. Not everyone is on social media. Not everyone reads AccountingWeb. Not everyone belongs to a Facebook community group. Not everyone is watching webinars. Something I've seen over the last nine months is that people really do learn [about the tools] for the very first time when they have a face-to-face conversation.

So even though the pandemic was a catalyst and accelerator for digital adoption by small business owners because they went from paper-based payments to a cashless society, mobile apps, Teams, and Zoom. Even though some accountants picked up new skills or new ways of working, it was still not a great experience for those who actually learn from others, who benefit from that face-to-face, approach. Maybe they all need to see it happening in real time.

A challenge

Tech take-up and desirability is more than just features. There is still a need for further improvement, especially in respect of first use and digitally guided set-up. If we go back in time to the pandemic, there was a surge of interest towards cash flow management. We could see the chat on social media. What did they want to use? Fluidly? Float? Futrli? Fathom? People would say, "Oh, no, I just want to use an excel spreadsheet". Why? Because the business didn't have their current financial information to hand. The fast track approach was to drop some bank data into Excel – analyse, categorise, and then model what-ifs. This was time consuming, costly to maintain and prone to inaccuracies. Just imagine the value and reduction in workload if clients were presented with an app which was intuitive to set-up, guided them to connect their bank feed and gave them (and you) the confidence for them to categorise their first expense? Fast forward, that is now a reality, which means the accountant can spend their time on advising rather than processing.

The game changing tech exists, the demand exists, but still adoption is slow. I believe the other challenge to be resolved is awareness. Not everyone is on social media. Not everyone reads AccountingWeb. Not everyone belongs to a Facebook community group. Not everyone is watching webinars. Something I've seen and experienced during 2022 is that people really do learn [about the tools] for the very first time when they have a face-to-face conversations.

Though the pandemic was a catalyst and accelerator for digital adoption by small business owners because they went from paper-based payments to a cashless society, mobile apps, Teams, and Zoom. Even though some accountants picked up new skills or new ways of working, it was still not a great experience for those who learn and are inspired by others, who benefit from conversation over email comms or digital communities. The power and benefit of seeing tech in action, in real time cannot be overvalued."

> **Will to learn – correlation of clarity of purpose with direction and success**
> I talk about purpose a lot, these days. But it's only in the last two or three years that I've been able to correlate the clarity of Farnell Clarke's purpose with our consistency of direction and success. I wonder if it's only something that you can see clearly with hindsight.

The take-home

The accountancy sector as a whole has been strangely slow to fully adopt cloud accounting. This leaves great potential opportunity for firms that do so now, and is a long term recipe for disaster for those that do not, because their clients will move to accountants that can provide faster value added services.

Why you should never forget your purpose

12

Purpose, the Underlying Driver

THEN

"The firm has seen consistent growth averaging 36 per cent year on year for the last 10 years."

NOW

"Thinking backwards, I realise explicitly that it was the clarity of my original idea that drove our purpose, which in turn drove the firm's ongoing success."

It's quite funny because you don't think about it as it happens, but having the right start point is essential. The day before you start a new venture, when you say to your self "right, I'm going to set this up. I'm going to do it in this way and it's going to change the world," is more important than you know.

The more I think about purpose the more convinced I am that the fundamental driver for my firm – an essential contribution to our success – is down to the clarity of purpose. With the benefit of hindsight, knowing – clearly knowing – our purpose; why we do what we do, what drives our decisions, how we want to be thought of and who we want to be, keeps us on track. For me, it was about changing the way professional services were perceived and the way they were delivered. It informed – and still informs – how we grow our firm, how we respond to new challenges and how we relate to ideas. It was vital in creation of our performance management structure and in more things than I can count. My laser focus on purpose – the whole time since the firm was an idea I was developing – has been the single most valuable thing we've had.

Diagram adopted from the concept of Ikigai

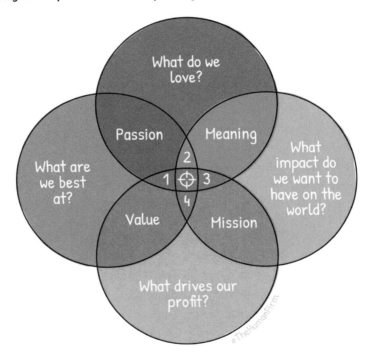

Key:

1 – Profit now,

2 – Most Accountants (client insights for free),

3 – Short termist client benefits,

4 – Stuck! Unscalable processes mean firm never reaches its potential.

The relationship between strategy, vision, values and purpose

Strategy is a plan of action designed to achieve a specific goal or set of goals. It outlines the steps a business will take (its route map) to achieve its objectives and includes the allocation of resources, the identification or risk and opportunities and the implementation of tactics (lower level route maps and sometimes project plans).

A strong strategy will help the firm achieve its vision and values, and through that deliver on its purpose. The vison outlines what the firm wants to achieve in the future, the values represent the principles that guide the firms actions, and the purpose defines why the firm exists.

A good strategy will consider the firm's strengths and weaknesses as well as the opportunities and threats in its external environment. It aligns with the vision, values and purpose so that the firm effectively executes its mission while remaining true to its guiding principles.

Your strategy will include the transition through fully cloud-based to human firm, and may involve the development of all or some of the things I am discussing in this book.

Delivering professional services in a different, better way

Strategy, vision and values are all vital. At the time of writing the last book – when it was not yet possible to be as fully cloud-based as I'd have liked – I talked about how becoming fully digital was a vital step in our strategy. We've come a long way since then, and it is only in the last two or three years that I've been able to correlate our clarity of purpose to our success. I set up Farnell Clarke to deliver professional services in a different, better way. I wanted to change the way professional services were delivered and the way in which they were perceived by users of those services. It's why we adopted the tech. It's why we priced what we did the way we did. The reason we did all the other things that we did was that our purpose was so clear.

"

> *Clearly knowing our purpose: why we do what we do, what drives our decisions, how we want to be thought of and who we want to be, keeps us on track.*

"

James Ashford told me about GoProposal's purpose, embedded in a core value; "At GoProposal, one of our core values was "Demonstrate that you care." Caring isn't enough. It has to be demonstrated because the client has to feel cared for. It all comes back to feelings. You could do something behind the scenes that shows you care, but the phone call to the client to tell them what you've done is what they see, the demonstration."

Knowing who you want to care for is important too, and inextricably tied up with your purpose. As Eleanor Shakeshaft said; "Somehow we get apologetic for the type of firm we want to be. We worry it will alienate people. In fact it is probably the opposite, we start to attract the right people if we are clear about who we are and what we want."

*Your purpose informs
the client proposition,
drivers and enablers,
while the hub supports it*

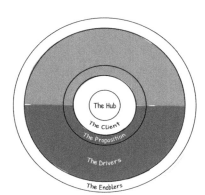

*How do we approach
the evolution of the
Human Firm*

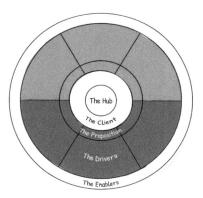

*Human Firm drivers, with vision
and purpose as the foundation
and experience building trust –
with clients and staff alike*

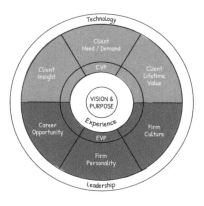

People, purpose and success

In a world in flux, Millennial and GenZ members increasingly see employment flexibility as essential. Post crises, and in the current age of rapid technological change and business model disruption, firms have begun to find themselves caught between Covid and compliance requirements needing radical adaptation, employees who no longer see themselves in jobs for life and clients whose expectations are constantly shifting. To navigate that, they need to clearly articulate the purposes that may have in the past been merely implicit for internal and external stakeholders alike.

As baby boomers age out, and new generations of clients and potential employees become the majority, the clear articulation and demonstration-by-doing of a firm's purpose is increasingly important. And it should be. One of the most important contributions to society of any business – including that of accountancy – is driving sustainable, long-term growth whilst investing in solutions for future challenges.

The accounting world may be slow to adopt such a thing, but we should take a note of what is happening elsewhere. Companies with an established sense of purpose – one that is measured in terms of social impact such as community growth and not just the bottom-line figures – outperformed the S&P 500 by 10 times between 1996 and 2011. It's a cognitive jump, but a necessary one. When I mentor people in other accounting firms they normally get me in because they think they want to talk about technology or process. Without fail, we end up talking about purpose. Purpose informs vision, it informs values and it informs pricing. All things that accountants generally don't do well. And once we can clearly articulate our purpose we know the importance of keeping a weather eye on the rest of the world because trends and developments elsewhere can help us move towards our purpose and help us better serve our clients.

Meanwhile, the number of BCorp certified companies tripled between 2016 and 2021, in 2021, 80 per cent of people polled by Sizzle (a fintech-company) said that they would pay more for a sustainable product and 81 per cent that ethics were an important aspect of their purchasing decisions. We ignore these trends at our peril. In fact, if we're operating as a business we can't ignore them at all.

Will to learn – communicate your purpose

It turns out that was one of the biggest mistakes we made in the original de-Willing scaling process was that I was out of the loop in terms of talking to new joiners. Then James Kay started to leave other people to do the interviews and I think new joiners lost the sense of what we are really about. We discovered how quickly things can change if you stop talking about the things that are really important.

And there's more. By coming out of the interview process entirely without ensuring that our values were communicated from the outset, people came into the firm with different expectations. We also wonder if others, who decided not to take up offers, might have been enthusiastic to join us had we been clearer on our purpose, vision and values from the outset.

So now I am talking to every new joiner. We talk through Farnell Clarke's values, about our vision and of course about our purpose. And while it is in a way, a stepping back in to do work I thought I had left, it is also about creating a new process for the scaled and scaling firm, with the things I have to do.

B Corporation

BCorp or B Corporation is a private certification of for-profit companies of their 'social and environmental performance' distinct from any legal definition. Organisations become BCorp accredited because it shows clients and staff that they meet the highest verified standards of social and environmental performance, public transparency and legal accountability.

A challenge

A recent McKinsey study found that 70 per cent of employees said their sense of purpose is defined by their work. It makes sense then that a firm's purpose should be defined by its impact on the future and by an idea of how we want our staff and clients to feel. If that is so, it should indeed inform everything we do.

Establishing your purpose

Every person, every firm and every company has a purpose (although multi-partner purposes like their personality may be schizophrenic). However, to articulate your firms purpose it has to first be established.

Purpose needs to be people driven. It must be real, alive and something that everyone will adopt, exhibit and embrace. So, to discover your firm's purpose, engage its people – and its key stakeholders – in discovering what that is.

When doing so, make sure it is within the broader context of the firm's personalities, brand and vision. That said, like discovering most things at a deep, firm-wide level, it is a long process based on a series of questions around what you love, the impact you want to leave in the world, what you want to drive profit and what you want to be best at.

Here are the purpose statements of some non accounting firms that might inspire you:

AirBnB:
'Creating a world where Anyone can Belong Anywhere.'

Tesla:
'To accelerate the world's transition to sustainable energy.'

Patagonia:

'We're in business to save our home planet.'

LinkedIn:

'Create economic opportunity for every member of the global workforce.'

You'll see from this that grand aspirations are great starters, and the important thing is to be authentic, follow the purpose that you believe in and don't worry about how your purpose sounds to others. These are all huge goals that might sound a little arrogant. I guess that me on my own in 2007 wanting to change the way professional services were delivered might have sounded that way too.

The take-home

Purpose is an articulation of motivation. It includes how people in the firm do things, the impact the firm wants to make and how the firm wants stakeholders to interact and perceive it.

A clear purpose will help everyone in the firm understand what to do and how to do it. It is an essential sustainability and development tool and will help us understand how to react to unplanned situations.

A new way to think
about your clients
(at least for accountants)

13

Client Lifetime Value

THEN

"The best thing about being an accountant is gross recurring fees and the worst thing about being an accountant is gross recurring fees. They set the bar really low, because all we've got to do to get paid is not screw up. Where is the motivation to do more?"

NOW

"But clients are changing, and the owners of those firms that don't change now will wake up one day to discover that their clients have moved on."

> **Client Lifetime Value**
>
> There are many definitions of Client Lifetime Value (CLV), often known as Lifetime Value (LTV). We calculate it by multiplying the value of the customer to the business by their average lifespan. Different clients and different sectors can have different average lifespans. Others factor in gross margin, operational expenses and even marketing expenses.

Once we've established our practice, and got some clients, those gross recurring fees that pay for our clients' compliance keep on coming. Unless we screw up, for a certain period of time – the client lifetime - our clients keep coming back.

We know the average client stays for seven to ten years, so can calculate our client lifetime value. To make things easy, if a client with a £5,000 a year fee stays for ten years, the client lifetime value (CLV) is £50,000. Does this change the way you think about that client? I believe it should.

Go into a Citroen dealership, and they might offer you a cup of coffee that will most likely be in a paper cup and from a machine. And that is fine. However, go to a BMW dealership and your coffee will be freshly made by a barista in the showroom's coffee bar. That client experience is related to the potential value of what you'll be spending; between £8,000 and £40,000 for a Citroen and between £30,000 and over £150,000 for a BMW. Client experience in both cases are related to the potential value of the purchases.

We should be conscious of the investment that people are making in us. £50,000 of a client's hard-earned money is a sizeable sum. Understanding how you add to their value (and yes, they to yours) at a process level, along with how the pod adds to the value at a lifetime value level becomes key.

So what does that tell us about how we should think of our client experience? Well quite a bit. You'd be far more willing to invest in a potential client that delivered you £50,000 over 10 years than just £500 over one.

That is just the beginning. A client that is consistently happy with your services is unlikely to leave you. It's common sense, and financially worthwhile. Finding ways to provide extra client happiness might enable you to extend client lifetime as well as the value. After all, great service and £75,000 over 15 years sounds a lot better than £50,000 over 10!

THE HUMAN FIRM by WILL FARNELL

NPS

Net Promoter® Score (NPS) is a client satisfaction and service quality metric based on a single survey question that asks accounting clients **how likely they are to recommend your firm to a friend or colleague**. Clients respond using a numeric scale of zero to 10, ten being extremely likely and zero being not likely at all.

It is calculated by taking the percentage of detractors from the percentage of promoters, and is unique as it provides a standardised way of measuring and reporting on client satisfaction and service quality that can be applied at any level; the accounting industry as a whole or per sector, at firm level, within practice area and even by type of client.

Average net promoter score over eight years for accountancy sector
Source: ClearlyRated 2022

	2014	2015	2016	2017	2018	2019	2020	2021	2022
Net Promoter Score	31	31	28	18	19	24	23	38	39
Average Score	8.03	8.13	8.02	7.67	7.63	7.99	7.85	8.16	8.30
% Promoters	49%	51%	48%	43%	43%	45%	43%	53%	50%
% Passives	33%	29%	33%	32%	33%	34%	38%	33%	39%
% Detractors	18%	20%	20%	25%	24%	21%	19%	15%	11%

Client Retention

"

It's not enough to wait for the clients to ask for what they want because in today's climate they're more likely to Google a firm that says they can and simply go.

"

Winning a client is far easier than retaining them, and as Helen Cockle says; "you can't retain a customer just by what you're doing today, because in a year's time some other upstart will come along and offer far more and your client will be gone. And it's very easy to pick up your bags and switch at the moment."

Client lifetime value challenge

In a recent conversation, Helen pointed out that we have got to start thinking about client behaviour in the same way that SAAS businesses do. She got quite excited at my suggestion that we couldn't give good insight 20-years-ago, but now can because we have the data and the tools, and we discussed client lifetime value, (and why many accountants don't use it), and how tech, forecasting, and a change of mindset is vital. It's not enough to wait for the clients to ask for what they want, because in today's climate they're more likely to google a firm that says they can and they'll just go.

Different perspectives

It's certainly a mindset. In the early years of Farnell Clarke, between around 2009 and 2013 I would go to speak at events. The interesting thing was, almost without exception 90 per cent of the audience who were at the early adopter or innovator stage had not trained in practice. They were largely from a commercial background, and were management accountants, industry accountants or had perhaps trained in practice then gone into industry. This left them open to a very different way of working and leads us back to our purpose, vision and values.

With a clear purpose, vision and values, you will be able to articulate your client value proposition, (and employee value proposition too). In our world this needs clearly defined statements. 'This is what we do and how we do it' because once we understand that, and the demand that goes with it, we can get to the rest through the depth of relationship with our clients, since that helps us understand what our clients need.

Lifetime value is a business decision. While the old practice view is of clients being just the one annual fee, if we look at the figures as a business we can consider how to increase our CLV by extending the client life and identifying other services that can make a difference. Knowing the true value of the average new customer is more than the original year's fee, you are likely to be prepared to pay a lot more than competitors who aren't thinking in this way. Examining CLV between different client segments may take you in unexpected new directions and simply increasing the cost of customer acquisition might enable you to make offers or provide services that others firms would not consider.

Record background

Stefan Barrett has a different perspective on Client Lifetime Value. Inspired by his experience working for the fast-growing Rekordelig (the Swedish cider company), his firm, Bee Motion serves clients that turn over less than two million. Once they reach that level, Bee Motion will channel them elsewhere. However, the suite of services his firm is offering maximises CLV when he has them.

Will to learn – in house human resources

We started offering in-house HR because it works seamlessly with our payroll services.

It's kind of one of those no-brainer services because if you're already running a payroll for clients you are already aware when a client takes on a first member of staff or an additional member of staff. It's really easy at that time to ask the client if they'd like help with an employment contract, if they have an employee handbook, are there other HR obligations they need to fulfil that we can help with technology for. It's just a really simple way of extending an offering. It even lends itself to recurring revenue, so you can put retainers in place with your clients, and just take your payroll bureau just a little bit further.

We tested this with the white-labelled external consultant for a number of years, and relatively recently made the jump and recruited a senior HR director into Farnell Clarke. As well as managing our internal HR she is building an external service line and bringing in some operational HR people to help deliver that on a day to day basis.

This is a great demonstration of expanding existing offerings by adding slightly different products.

Why is CLV important to your firm?

- You can't improve what you don't measure, at least not consistently,

- It helps you make more accurate financial predictions for your firm and better marketing strategy decisions,

- It helps you see more clearly whether you should do something to improve client relationships,

- Studies have shown that existing customers spend 67 per cent more than new customers, so it makes sense to find ways to extend your client lifetime,

- Conventional wisdom indicates that keeping existing clients can cost five times less than attracting new ones,

- Existing clients are more likely to buy. The probability of selling to existing customers is 60-70 per cent while selling to a new customer is just five to 20 per cent. Increasing your client retention rate by just five per cent increases profits by 25-95 per cent,

- By focusing on CLV your firm will be at a competitive advantage, since about 50 per cent companies put greater focus on customer aquisitions with 18 per cent on retention.

Challenges involving CLV

- It can be hard to measure since it needs good KPIs and (ideally) real time tracking,
- High level results may be misleading, since it can cover problems in certain segments.

The take-home

- Clients are changing, and a deepening of relationship may increase your CLV,
- The same deepening relationship may enable you to provide value added services and client insights,
- Customer Lifetime Value (CLV) is a measure of the average customers' revenue generated over their entire relationship with the firm,
- Comparing CLV to customer acquisition cost is a quick method of estimating a client's profitability and the business's potential for long term growth,
- Considering how to extend CLV can increase growth irrespective of the number of a firm's clients,
- Looking at CLV by customer segment may provide new insights into what does – and does not – working for your firm.

Notes

PART FOUR

MAKING IT HUMAN

**How to think of the human firm,
what and why – the nub.**

This section talks about the value of good data and how data is valueless unless it's providing great client insights, about shifting your mindset from compliance only to compliance-plus, about how this changes as the expectations of clients change, about the importance of culture, personality and experience for clients and staff alike. It examines the importance of culture and personality, the usefulness of the Net Promoter Score as a tool, and the relevance of establishing the right number of customer touchpoints. It looks at how Making Tax Digital and Know Your Clients can be used as both excuse and bootstrap for change. Finally it talks about how you should use this book to get better client insights.

Tech is the means,
not the end.

14

Making it Human

THEN

"Firstly, delivering great services; secondly, incorporating great tech to continue delivering these great services; thirdly, using tech to extract a better quality of data for analysis; and finally, using all this to give great customer experience."

NOW

"Client Experience is (still) King."

Way back before we adopted automated data entry software, clients were pretty relaxed about getting records in, and our post would sometimes include documents that were more than 18-months-old. I knew it would be how we used the tech, the availability of data and promptness of suggestions related to it that would be key. There's more about that in The Digital Firm.

Practice doesn't make perfect

Great data delivers nothing on its own. To do right by our clients through delivering great insights, we also need to understand their ambitions. Once we know whether they want to become very rich, to be the best, to have more time for their family or to make a difference, we are part of the way towards understanding what insights might be useful to them. Even all of that is useless without empathy, which is lucky because that's one thing AI, machine learning or any other new tech can not provide.

To support the insights that we deliver through empathy, we need processes that enable great communications between us. They need to be set up with good control of tech-people interactions and in ways that help us deepen our understanding of our clients and our perceived availability and utility so that our mutual relationship can grow. And make no mistake, our client relationships must grow. Remember what I said about gross recurring fees being both the best and the worst thing for a firm? Far from making things perfect, practising the same thing without change will lose them in the end. This is true whether or not you go for pure compliance or compliance-plus. Change that both benefits and is communicated between you and your client must be integrated into your practice, implemented and talked about in useful, achievable ways.

Knowing where you're going is only half the battle

Providing you are focused on developing better services, insights and added value for clients, and you're looking at your firm as a business rather than a practice, you'll have a good idea of where you're going.

"

> *Fast data, well considered processes and good client communications are vital foundations on which you can build the fully Human Firm.*

"

Sadly while some firms have the right idea, their execution doesn't match up. It has to start with up-to-date data of good quality, (yes, that goes back to daily bookkeeping again), end-to-end cloud-based processes, (as described in The Digital Firm), continue through a good level of communication with your client, include regular, ongoing and consistent assessments as to how services can add to the client's value without overwhelming or annoying them and develop in ways that support the clearly defined targets. Since you need to work with your client on a human basis all year round, it goes without saying that if you're not already fully cloud-based you need to accelerate the transition. Fast data, well considered processes and good client communications are vital foundations on which you can build the fully Human Firm.

Fast Data – Change your mindset

I've said it before and I'll say it again. Why would you possibly think that monthly or quarterly bookkeeping is good and the right thing to do? You would never do that if you were a financial controller, finance manager or bookkeeper working in an organisation. So why do you think it's okay today for your clients? Much better to consider what has to change to make daily bookkeeping work.

Reflecting the whole business model shift from compliance to service means we should always be looking for an opportunity to give clients better data. So whether we do it alone, create app stacks to support it or have the apps and need better processes, every change stems from the need to control the quality and timeliness of data.

This is fundamentally important if you want to become a fully Human Firm so it bears repeating. Since we want to be able to talk to our client all year round and have valuable interactions, we need up to date data. This enables us to use data to help them while looking both inwards and outwards, and to identify other services we could deliver. This in turn is only possibly by delivering existing services more efficiently, which in turn is only possible once we control the data.

From regular gathering of quality data through client insights and better understanding to more revenue, as previously described.

So how do we use people process and technology to ensure that clients get the right data in a timely manner that lets them make the decisions they need to? It's in my last book under the heading 'The Biggest Issue'. It kind-of hasn't changed. Most people still haven't worked out how to deliver timely, good quality data. Even some of the firms that I'm working are struggling to get it right. They're making great progress, but not to the point where they're doing it for all of their clients. It's still a really big issue.

How accounting firms who know that they can use client data to give clients better insight get it wrong

1. **Lack of technical expertise:** Many accounting firms may not have the necessary technical expertise to properly analyse and interpret large amounts of data.

2. **Data quality issues:** Data may be inaccurate, incomplete, or inconsistent, which can lead to unreliable insights.

3. **Data security concerns:** Client data may contain sensitive information that must be protected, which can be a challenge for firms without proper security measures in place.

4. **Lack of investment:** Investing in technology and resources for data analysis may not be a priority for some firms, which can hinder their ability to effectively use client data.

5. **Difficulty integrating data from multiple sources:** Data from different sources may not be easily integrated, which can limit the ability to see a comprehensive view of the client's financial situation.

6. **Insufficient data analysis skills:** The ability to analyse and interpret data effectively is a critical skill that not all accountants may possess.

7. **Inadequate data visualization tools:** Poor visualization tools can make it difficult to communicate insights effectively to clients.

8. **Resistance to change:** Some accountants may be resistant to new technologies and approaches to data analysis, making it challenging to effectively utilize client data.

9. **Limited understanding of client needs:** Without a deep understanding of a client's needs, it may be difficult to determine what insights are most valuable.

10. **Inadequate focus on actionable insights:** Providing insights that are not actionable or relevant to the client's business can be a waste of time and resources for both the firm and the client.

Changing comparisons

Making your firm as human as possible means we can't just compare ourselves to other accountants. Modern consumers – particularly millennials and GenZ – have grown up with different expectations. And while we don't have to compete with Amazon, we do need to consider it. Amazon has changed expectations around what convenience is, what speed of delivery is acceptable and what customer experience should be.

The take-home

Unsurprisingly, real-time human, communications are essential to the Human Firm. To support this you need real-time data and to support that you need control of the bookkeeping.

Good client relationships,
great experiences, and
barriers to exit

15

Culture, Personality and Experience

THEN

"It's true that extra costs are incurred in subscriptions, and many of the add-ons cost a little extra, but I believe the advantages to your clients and your practice far outweigh these costs."

NOW:

"Costs will be outweighed by the benefits that you deliver. You'll have happier clients, greater efficiency, you'll most likely be extending your CLV and will have automated the mundane."

The virtuous circle

If you have good relationships with your clients you'll be providing a great client experience, and if you have great client experiences you'll generally have good relationships. It's not just that the best interactions complete the virtuous circle, but that in maintaining both you are creating barriers to exit. Your clients will be getting so much from you – and appreciating it – that most will not be motivated to move. The few that do look around will find it hard to match what you offer.

> **"**
> *If the vast majority (I mean 70 per cent plus) of new business is not from referrals we need to take a look in the mirror!*
> **"**

For your client, it's about transitions. We need clients to understand the value of transitioning from sporadic to daily bookkeeping, to understand how access to up-to-date online ledgers benefits them, to understand that their regular chats with their firm representative give value, insights, a safe place to talk and more. At Farnell Clarke we know this is possible because our clients understand these things already.

But mutual warm-and-fuzzies aren't sufficient. We need to actually think about the proactive measurement of client opinion. Such measurements are valuable from the point of view of making sure they're happy with the communications and services we're offering, and from a marketing point of view too. Your promoters are the people who will be referring your firm and your services to everybody else. In other words if you want a business that is going to grow easily, having a whole bunch of promoters in your client base is going to generate new business on a regular basis, without you having to think about it. That's where NPS comes in. If the vast majority (I mean 70 per cent plus) of new business is not from referrals we need to take a look in the mirror!

How NPS helps

The NPS helps companies maintain customer satisfaction and increase the quality of client relationships by providing insights into how customers perceive the brand, products and services. A high score indicates a high level of customer satisfaction and loyalty which can be used to identify areas or strength and success. A low NPS score indicates areas where the company needs to improve its customer experience and build stronger relationships with its clients.

By regularly surveying clients and asking them to rate the likelihood of recommending the business, your firm can make informed decisions regarding improvement. It's important to choose the area of assessment well. Whether responsiveness to client communications, quality of service and support, or usefulness of insights offered, each NPS value provides both a touchpoint and decision point on which the need for improvement can be assessed, planned and provided.

With great growth comes great responsibility

Karen Kennedy of Kennedy Accountancy has a strong community purpose. It is expressed in everything that her firm does, in what clients she accepts and what she doesn't. She concentrates on clients who live on or close to her remote Scottish location close to the Isle of Skye, gives financial incentives to local businesses that haven't won grant funding and is providing local training for people who would only otherwise get it by moving away.

Back to basics

All of this goes back to the idea of providing value to clients, and reflects the choice I had already made about running a business rather than a practice. Consider your likely CLV and how you might use NPS to extend it. If you think like a business you will understand there will be costs. They will be outweighed by the benefits because you're going to have happier clients, greater efficiency, you'll most likely be extending your CLV and will have automated the mundane. On top of all of this, your team will be happier because they're not doing dull work. The end result is well-worth the investment.

Ultimately though, our thinking starts and stops with the service we deliver for our clients. If we're giving a client what they really want then we're giving them a better service. It might be better because they want things we've not discussed, or because they've not understood how other insights might be useful, or it simply because we haven't spent the time with them to find out.

Will to learn – don't sweat over your NPS

For a long time I was in two minds about undertaking an NPS survey. On one hand, I was desperate for some good metrics. On the other hand, as I knew we weren't delivering the kind of service that I wanted, I was scared. I managed to convince myself to put it off from mid-2016 all the way to February 2019 when I felt we had cracked the delivery of excellent service. What we lost through my procrastination was the ability to clearly see the progress we had made. While we knew where we had got to, we didn't have the start point quantified. Our NPS was 72 in 2019. In 2016 we might have been at 30 which would not have been that bad. With no baseline, we weren't as clear as we could have been on our progress. In retrospect we should have given our clients the opportunity to say bad things because we could have shown them being fixed. Because of this my advice is to get your baseline sorted. That way you can recognise and celebrate the successes when you achieve them. And don't sweat it. Your estimate of the NPS will always be lower than it really is.

Will to learn – culture and personality

The Post-Covid Great Resignation is more like a Great Reshuffle. People move around, and even rotate. We've had staff that left and came back because the grass wasn't greener after all, so we know that culture is more important than ever.

The combination of our culture and personality provides an element of consistency and relatability that goes beyond mere brand. Culture is relatively static and tends to remain consistent over time, while personality reflects the environment, (both internal and external), in which the firm exists at a time. Personality therefore helps to differentiate a brand from its competitors and make it more relatable to the target audience.

A well-defined personality expresses our firm's shared purpose. It helps to align Farnell Clarke members with the firm's value and make them feel more invested in our success. It also helps ensure that all staff members know how to communicate. As part of this at our monthly, all-staff town halls I remind staff to imagine how our clients will feel before sending any communication at all.

By the same token, it helps create a more engaging and memorable client experience, helps build trust and credibility and helps our clients feel more connected. It helps to resonate between different generations of clients as well as different market segments. One client left when we put a pub in our office. That's fine, they'll most likely be happier with more traditional accountants. Meanwhile our professionalism, expertise and experience will draw typical GenXers, our innovation and authenticity will draw more GenZ and Millenials and our uniqueness, our personalisation and responsiveness will appeal in particular to GenZs. That these are aspects of Farnell Clarke's personality, informed by our purpose is for us, a natural thing.

Taking it personally – with Stefan Barrett

After a recent conversation about branding and firm personality, (see appendix), Stefan consulted his clients and staff, and developed this.

1) Culture

a. Accountability – taking ownership of tasks, the team knowing the importance of their role. Intrapreneurship attitude is influential throughout the team.

b. Approachable – no judgement with any questions or uncertainty, able to ask anyone for help. Driven team, building a network of support internally and to our clients acting like more of a business partner than just your standard grey suit, red tie cliché.

c. Strategic mindset – Strategic thinking can help the team go beyond simply balancing the books and instead help clients understand the bigger picture, identify opportunities for growth, and achieve their business goals.

2) Brand

a. Personalised service – Our personalised service is rooted in a humanised approach, where we strive to provide financial solutions that meet the unique needs of each client. We take pride in understanding our clients' perspective and running their business as if it were our own, (essentially, stepping in their shoes).

b. Trustworthy – 'Honey being money and bees looking after it' not only provides a creative and memorable messaging but also reinforces Bee Motion's commitment to being trustworthy. Just like bees are known for their diligence and honesty in protecting their hive, Bee Motion aims to protect and manage their clients' finances with the same level of care and responsibility.

c. Vision – Our focus is helping our clients look forward and not backwards. We strive to continuously leverage technology to reduce the overall burden of their financial affairs. By sharing the same vision as our clients, we aim to help them achieve their goals and aspirations.

3) Personality

a. Inclusivity – At Bee Motion, inclusivity is a top priority. The company's tech-driven approach does not exclude anyone, as we are dedicated to tailoring our services to meet the unique needs of all clients, regardless of their age, background, or tech-savviness. Bee Motion creates a supportive environment, making everyone feel valued and included. We believe everyone deserves access to quality accounting services, regardless of their circumstances.

b. Passion and excitement – Passion and excitement are at the forefront of the company culture. Despite owning the business, Stefan maintains a hands-on approach and is present in the office daily, setting an example to his team. There is a strong emphasis on hard work and equal distribution of tasks, with no hierarchy present. This creates a dynamic and enthusiastic environment that permeates throughout the entire firm.

Will to learn – communicating culture is key

We stopped communicating directly to staff on a regular basis after Covid because we brought in a leadership team and thought they'd do it. We now do a town hall every month. Once a month, I apologise. Every single month. I say, "put yourself in the shoes of the client. Before you send that email, before you pick up the phone to have a conversation, put yourself in the shoes of the client and listen to what you're going to say to them. How does that make you feel? How might you respond? How might you react?"

Both the town hall with staff and the reminders are vital, because they help us remember our firms culture, our personality and that what most matters is our clients.

Pledge one per cent
Started by Salesforce, Atlassian and Rally, Pledge one per cent is a global corporate philanthropy movement that engages business leaders and their employees to give back to local and national social causes through an ongoing commitment of staff time, product, and/ or cash derived from the company's profits or equity.

Personality, Purpose and Profitability – Conversation with James Lizars, Founder and CEO of Thrive Accountants

My conversation with James Lizars covered sustainability, purpose and profitability. What struck me most was in the consistency of how his thinking determined his firm's personality.

"I'd say that we are not dissimilar to a lot of Progressive partner practices. My background is in industry, in the advertising industry as an agency FD, and I started this business up in 2013 off the back of observing the opportunity with Xero, and being able to bring my skills and experience alongside those tools and technologies to help smaller businesses get the full advantage of a finance function many many years before they can afford it through the old recruitment way.

We've grown from that base. We're now a team of seven, and we have a focus on early stage technology businesses, providing them with a full finance, function and compliance. I guess you'd call it a pillar of what they need. We try to do the whole piece for them, so they don't need any other finance professional involved.

Going back to my agency days, I was a huge champion of employee engagement initiatives within the business. Because an accounting firm – similarly to a creative or advertising agency type firm – has a business where the product is only as good as the people. Essentially you get to recruit and retain the best talent by treating them well, and by making sure they get out of the relationship what they are seeking, which is generally more than just money.

I think it is true that employee engagement has been a driver of growth profitability, and commercial outcomes in the last couple of decades. There is plenty of academic research to back this assertion up. In the coming decades this will surely be proven and pushed more, so that more purposeful businesses that work on something beyond profit will become more important to employees.

When you start to stare at it closely enough, you think, "well, actually, it's just about people and people like this stuff beyond profit. Therefore surely it's going to attract, not repel other businesses too, all other things being equal." If two businesses are identical, and one's doing something good in the world as well as making profit, then that's the one that's going to be more attractive.

I was looking at this in the context of the one per cent pledge, which is one per cent of time, products, and profit. And I thought, "that doesn't feel that much of a give from me. What if it was one per cent of revenue? Surely we can swing enough buying decisions to get that back?" I sort of played with this brain toy for a bit, trying to work it out commercially. Then, long story short, we went on a bit of a journey with it.

We fully embraced BCorp because we were kind of doing most of it anyway. A big segment of it is employee engagement, another segment of it is not being wasteful and a digital practice has very few outputs other than work. So it wasn't much of a reach. Actually, one of the big component parts was dialing up the giving piece to 20 per cent of profit. That became our stake in the ground, and it's one of the big things that makes us different to a lot of businesses, businesses who are, just run by nice people doing good things for clients.

ras
a**The One Million Tree Pledge**
The Million Tree Pledge is a **group of businesses and ambitious individuals who have come together to take action and do something radical in response to the climate emergency**. Each pledger has made a bold, two-part commitment to plant over one million trees by a specific date. Most pledgers have chosen 2030.

Also, along the way, we did the One Million Tree pledge. I was looking at our journey to net zero, and thinking, "well in 2020, I bought carbon offsets to offset our entire footprint going back to when the practice was founded. It cost me than £500 ($605 or 570€). I was like, "OK, well, that doesn't feel like doing my bit for the environment". So I played around with what doing my bit was, looked at the privilege we have being born into in this country and thought, "well, there's all these people around the world that are going to feel the impacts worse than I will, so maybe I should do a bit more because of that. Then there's all these people around me who aren't really doing much of anything. They're just not there yet. So, if we actually want to make a difference, then people who are minded to need to pick up the slack of those who aren't". So I am not looking for climate neutral, which is £500 to offset our footprint.

I'm not even looking for Net Zero, that's really hard. The rules are different for small business, but in its purest form, you've got to reduce your emissions by 80 per cent, then you can offset. But reducing your emissions by 80 per cent is massively hard, because most of your emissions are in your supply chain like software vendors. I can't tell ... not just Xero, but Amazon ... that their AWS platform has to be on renewable energy, so that Xero can claim to be on their Net Zero journey, and therefore cover my emissions too. It's too hard. And our emissions are tiny anyway. So what is doing my bit?

Planting a shit load of trees. Yes, it's a lot money, but actually – again – it has a commercial basis. When I mapped it out, it was going to take about five per cent revenue which is just not a commercially sound decision. Then I thought, "what if we overlay growth? What growth rate do I need to do?" And that was pretty modest, about 20 per cent. And we are consistently achieving 30 per cent to 45 per cent, depending on what measure you use, so it's doable without being mad.

Therefore I asked myself how to leverage it to help it stimulate growth. We use it as a marketing tool unashamedly, because it's not just a marketing tool. It's something I want to do.

Will: It is a really interesting point. It is almost that a clarity of purpose is the by-product to growth and profitability. It's not marketing it's just communicating what you genuinely stand for and what you're genuinely striving to achieve.

James: Yes. And there are muddy puddles you can step in, all around this path. Claiming to be climate neutral or climate positive is one of those muddy puddles. Because it's usually used by people who don't understand what it really means and haven't done the hard yards. So to this day I still haven't made that claim.

But as long as you are stepping forward on this pathway with a degree of authenticity that is difficult to challenge, you can absolutely use it in your marketing communications and use it to attract and retain staff, customers and even engagement levels with suppliers. There's payoff as well.

I wouldn't say the climate path is our purpose. We are a pretty ordinary business in many ways. But most businesses are. This for me is where the win is. You've got the profit-at-any-cost-approach which is often standard. People I respect hugely say, "a business exists to make profit." They use that line constantly but it doesn't ring true. I've worked with lots of business owners over the years. Sure they may aim for profit, but it's an outcome, not what they set their business up for. It's not why they are making the choice to be a business owner, because it's hard.

It's not about the money, it's about what the money can do. And that's where the whole human factor comes in, because I would argue that it is different for everyone, as different as a fingerprint. There are only a handful of individuals, I would say, who are in it just for the money. Some of the most odious individuals in our society seem to use that money for their self esteem, or to have their collection of cars.

I'm not really in the market for a holiday home, or that kind of stuff. That's not what I want my life's work to be about. I've got young kids. This kind of started with the whole concept that they'll be teenagers about seven years from now. I can either run my firm trying to rinse profits, or I can do my bit for the planet. If I can say to my 13-year-old in seven years, "we planted a million trees, we did what we could," then I'm going to feel like I got a lot from my business. Meanwhile, you know… pension, house, holidays, a reasonable lifestyle… I cannot be a pauper who planted one million trees. That's just daft!

I think the final piece of it is that I'm using this platform to try to shift our industry in its thinking. Adopting a more BCorp minded approach to business is a perfectly valid commercial choice that can drive perfectly acceptable commercial outcomes.

Come 2030 I would say that we will have a body of evidence to prove causality between commercial outcome and purpose. I don't think it's there yet. If we can prove that using business as a force for good, whatever your version of good is, and if we can be giving permission to business owners to make more purposeful choices and pay for something that's not profitable in the knowledge and expectation that profit will more than likely follow. That's worth doing."

NPS and cognitive bias

Dr Roger Miles, visiting Lecturer, Advisor and Research Associate: Risk Perception, Regulatory Design, Public Trust and Governance at CSaP (the Cambridge Centre for Science and Policy) has a cautionary attitude towards NPS because of the cognitive biases involved. The alternative name for choice-supportive bias is post-purchase rationalisation, which gives you a clue about why he's cautions. It's the tendency to give a positive spin to a decision, and is hard to eliminate if we ask for NPS directly upon purchase or take-up of our service. That's because when people with this sort of bias choose one option over another, they are likely to downplay the bad aspects of their choice while amplifying any faults from the alternative. Confirmation bias, (the tendency to interpret new evidence as confirmation of one's existing beliefs or choices of theories), is something that we should also against. Accountants might ascribe a rise in NPS score to the wrong thing, while our clients might give us a higher NPS than we deserve because they've done so before and confirmation bias may be affecting them. With this in mind, think carefully about what you want to investigate with your NPS exercises, and make sure you're really investigating your objective.

Back to my own experience, where NPS has been extremely useful. I'd suggest any NPS is better than none at all, and – as with anything else – it makes sense to tweak it each time you use it.

The take-home

Culture and personality are important for both clients and staff alike. Clear understanding helps marketing, and makes the firm both more agile and relatable to all. NPS is a useful tool that helps understand which areas of the business might need improvement and as an overall check of the human-ness that your firm has achieved.

The potential
value of considered
communications

16

The Point of Touchpoints

"We're constantly looking for ways to use tech to free up staff time and develop more regular communications with clients to better understand our clients needs and provide better value-added services."

NOW

"We built a structure around team pods to ensure we create frequent and value-driven touchpoints with our clients so that we could develop great relationships and world class client experiences."

> **Touchpoints**
>
> A touchpoint is any time a potential or current customer comes in contact with you or your brand, before, during or after they are your client. Each touchpoint represents both risk and opportunity. An opportunity to listen and make improvements, or a risk to your reputation, profitability or simply because they've become annoyed.

Keeping it real

"How do I get a bounce-back loan? How do I pay furlough? What do I do because I've had to close?" During Covid, many of our team had their first experience of clients asking them for help beyond what they would normally do. It was a useful experience. Everyone started understanding that our clients really do value our input, that what we do is not just about compliance, and that our clients need our assistance.

I now find myself writing this book in the midst of a major cost of living crisis. There's huge uncertainty around the economy and – because there was support available during the pandemic – we're facing challenges far greater now than we were then. Our clients need us more than ever.

My first employee worked on payroll, at a time when we could have filed client payroll just once a year, (not according to payment cycles, as we have to now). At a time that most accountants would have seen such an action as a waste of time and hugely inefficient. I paid that person to send a payslip to every client once a month to create regular touchpoints. It worked. Quite often, a client would reply with something like "…by the way, can you help with this?" In taking the opportunity to deepen my relationships with my clients, I helped them provide opportunities for us.

When we first started working with one of our early tech partners in 2011 they came in to the office and helped us build a kind of onboarding team, (actually teams). They helped us think through how to successfully onboard a client, and got us to think clearly about how to create really great first impressions. We would not necessarily have done that, had they not spent time helping us think about onboarding and how that affected client success. Because our clients valued that process, it lead to better relationships. That probably lead to more recommendations too.

Mapping client touchpoints can be useful, whether it's to understand how they're feeling, to quantify effectiveness or to understand whether there are too many or too few. James Ashford suggests that a useful task is to map out the client touchpoints throughout the onboarding journey and to plot their feelings on a chart from crap to amazing. Plotting interactions against this can lead to useful results.

"

> *I love this, touchpoints are two way. The more we talk to clients, the more we learn and the more ideas we generate on how to help them. You can bet that the same questions will come up time and again. Once we help one client, it is only a matter of time before another client is in the same boat and straight off the bat we are equipped to help. Why have we not addressed to opportunity of building an arsenal of touchpoints?"* Eleanor Shakeshaft

"

Commonality, clients and communication

The commonality between these examples is in the touchpoints. The points of interaction between Farnell Clarke and its clients. The right steps in the right direction feel good and are enriching. Too few steps and the process becomes boring or meaningless. Too many and the audience gets simply turns off.

Back in 2007, 'online accountant' was considered a derogatory term for many. They thought we were trying to remove client contact to the absolute minimum whereas I felt the polar opposite was true. The internet had just become more than 'a thing' and I thought it amazing that there wasn't an opportunity to get to client data online. Why were we entering data in the corner of a cold dark room on a distant computer for which only one person had the key? I had this crazy idea that with internet based software, people could call me with questions and we could look at the same thing at the same time. I wanted to be closer to my clients, to encourage them to contact us more regularly and set up fixed fees so that they'd not be stopped by the idea of paying extra for those calls. I looked to online accounting to get 24/7 access to data to help me provide other people with the services, (and prices), I wanted for myself. I felt other accountancy practices missed the kind of service that enabled clients to just pick up the phone and ask. The kind of access I imagined was not for the old-style, stuck-thinking six-months-after-the-year-end-once-a-year service, but for whenever clients needed us.

Over time, as new online – and then cloud-based – apps became available, by carefully integrating client touchpoints into our processes, we ensured an increasingly mutually beneficial and mutually profitable relationship. A far cry from the derogatory online accountant term that others thought it would be.

James Ashford on Client Experience

Client Experience is more than just touchpoints

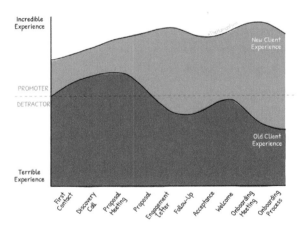

James has great perspective on client engagement, experience and touchpoints which is unsurprising considering his GoProposal background. Here's some of what he says:

- How your current clients talk about you. Do you make that predictable and encourage it?

- How you come across on your LinkedIn profile. Is your photo a professional one, or one of you at a party?

- Read the first words on your website. Are they about you or how you can help them?

- Their ability to book a call with you, when they're stressed out on a Sunday night, thinking about switching accountants,

- The first email you send confirming their meeting and whether it gets them excited about working with you,

- How easy it is to find your office. Are they driving round lost for ten minutes or have you sent them a short video of how to find you,

- The greeting they get at reception. Are they greeted by name, or does the receptionist have to ask who they are,

- The proposal meeting. Is their name on the screen and are they offered a menu to choose a drink from?

- Does the proposal meeting end on time, or do you allow it to overrun and thereby train this new, impressionable client that your time has no value,

- Your ability to produce a professional proposal, during the meeting. You've just told them you're a digital expert who will save them time, but if it takes you a day to get them a proposal, they'll think you don't know what you're talking about.

People can't judge you by what you say, but by what they experience.

The take-home

- Touchpoints have the potential for both risk and opportunity, as they can either make the client happy or harm the firm's reputation and profitability,

- When considering touchpoints, don't forget the ones that happen when you're not around,

- Careful development of client touchpoints strengthens your client relationship, enables your client to feel they can ask questions of you, and in doing so develops your business.

Why knowing
your client should
never be boring

17

Know your Client for Genuine Insight

THEN

"MTD gives us a reason for us to give clients for changing our services. This is a big incentive for us to update our offerings, deepen our relationships with our clients and lay down foundations for a thriving practice over the coming years. It's also what our clients want!"

NOW

"The biggest reason we need to adopt new business models to support our strategy to remain a leading-edge human firm is that it's what our clients want."

Since I wrote The Digital Firm we've had a huge increase in regulatory requirements, particularly for anti money laundering and Know Your Customer. For me, rather than using KYC as an opportunity to ask deeper questions that help us understand what our client is striving to achieve, we often get too focused on compliance. Whilst we have the regulatory obligation, let's use the opportunity that the obligation gives us to do something meaningful and valuable. That is, to understand what our clients are striving to achieve and how best we can support them in achieving their objectives.

Will to learn – KYC works

Know Your Customer (KYC) guidelines in financial services require that professionals make an effort to verify the identity, suitability, and risks involved with maintaining a business relationship. The procedures fit within the broader scope of a bank's anti-money laundering policy. They've been enshrined in law for years from Australia's AUSTRAC in 1989 to the UK's Money Laundering Regulations of 2017.

KYC standards involve several steps designed to verify the identity of clients, assess potential risks for money laundering, fraud, bribery, corruption and terrorism financing.

While we all understand the reasons behind Know Your Customer (KYC), and the time to use it as a catalyst is gone, it still provides a massive opportunity for firms to re-engineer and redesign their business while providing a justification for the clients to do so, since changes can be blamed on compliance requirements and the government. Firms that see KYC as a way of moving towards the Human Firm ideal, and of moving from accountancy practice to firm or business, will benefit hugely.

KYC, insightful insights and The Human Firm

As well as being a standard accountancy practice, KYC can be extended both through data analysis and genuine client interactions, to serve clients and firms more completely. While the suggestions below are examples, it's best to understand your own firm's clients and build extensions and new processes from there.

By collecting and analysing additional data, KYC can also give you a better understanding of your clients, enabling you to offer tailored services and chargeable insights.

Soft KYC practices might include;

- extension of client identity verification to determine principal stakeholders,
- assessment of the potential risk of money laundering or financing terrorism through the supply chain,
- assess supply chain regulatory compliance risks as well as that of the client,
- protection against financial crime while working with insurance,
- streamlining the client onboarding process,
- maintenance of clients' trust through good quality communications and timely data.

If we extend this to include information about clients' financial history, business operations and goals, this could be used to offer tailored services and chargeable insights such as financial forecasting, tax planning and risk management. Then, by employing digital tools and data analytics, firms could provide more insightful insights, and through this more value and better differentiation.

More views on KYC

In the same way as I had suggested in The Digital Firm, we can use KYC to expand our processes, systems and offerings. It is something that must be done. Clients understand this, so it gives us an 'in' to make changes. More than a critical aspect of ensuring regulatory compliance and managing risk, it becomes something useful, extends our Client Lifetime and facilitates a deeper, more useful and sustainable client relationship. Paraphrasing something that Karen Kennedy wrote recently;

"I'm probably somewhat different to most in that I already know, (in some way), around 80 per cent of my new clients. So a fair chunk of KYC as I see it is already underway. I collect some more information on the initial enquiry, then collect all the other boring stuff during their ID checks. I've linked them into an information gathering form. But I shorten it, as not everyone likes to tell their life story on a form. I'll follow up the initial enquiry for a discovery call. And I'm going to stop calling it that as I hate the term. Basically I want to humanise it more.

KYC means the opposite of what I was trained to think it meant. To me it means do I know what they want from their business? More importantly, do they know? What's their home life like? Who is at home? What is it that they are doing that serves our local community? It's not their NI number and address history. I'm also happy with the regulatory side of things. Doing things this way helps it flow as well as it can."

And paraphrasing Andrew Coulson from LinkedIn:

"It's an opportunity not only to check out that the client is legitimate and risk assess for AML compliance, but also to gather all the information necessary to start the client relationship off on the right footing. This could be by knowing names of their spouses, family, their financial background such as how made their money or were financed and more. That helps make sure we give the best advice and don't ask stupid questions. It also needs to be balanced against GDPR two.

Really getting to know your client is more than regulatory KYC by a long way. I just think it might be more efficient to do as part of the same workflow. A basic holistic getting to know the client, that you dig into later as part of the onboarding process, kick of meetings etc. Although if you did that, the downside would be a much longer period before signing off for KYC / AML approval."

View to a bill –
Conversation with Richard Bertin,
founder and CEO of All In Place

Will: The interesting bit for me about your perspective is your client facing approach about insights, client need versus demand, and client lifetime value. Following on from that, how do you see KYC; as a great opportunity, or mere compliance and risk profiling that enables us to show that we've done what we need to if the ICAEW or ACCA come along?

Richard: "It's fascinating to hear what you're talking about in the book. I'm 100 per cent on this in terms of what the profession should do.

As a qualified accountant I went into financial services in the UK and built a fee based practice with a value proposition for our clients before the Financial Services commission rules changed in 2013, 10 years ago. We segmented our clients, worked out the services that we should provide to different clients, and made sure that we charged appropriately.

Then there was a pivot moment for us, in the same way I think that the pivot moment is here now for the profession. The global financial crisis was phenomenal for the banks, because they just sold investment products. Nobody could do any wrong because the markets just went up and up. Then, all of a sudden, the market went down. All asset classes just sort of congregated together, and we sold a stake in our business to the family office of Flemings Bank (also the old James Bond family).

They realised that they needed an advisory proposition which was interesting in his own right. But the bit that became really interesting was when Fleming Family Office merged with a South African family office, called Stonehage. I had never heard of Stonehage at the time, and when I did a presentation at AccountingWeb recently and asked people there, nobody had heard of them either. Stonehage Fleming are now the largest independent family office in EMEA. They have 1,000 people and principal thing they do – is look after the business owner.

And of course, as business owners left South Africa, they went to America, and went to the UK. And the Stonehage business continued to assist, and they bought our financial planning business and had two law firms and private equity. So they effectively became a one stop shop for the business owner. They didn't do the sexy compliance stuff that accountants loved! But they did all those other things.

So now, we've gone through a pandemic. I wasn't in practice, but it must have been awful dealing with clients who were saying, "our businesses is going bust, we haven't got any money. What do we do with our staff?'"But we, the accounting profession, all sort of got through that. Then we have dreadful political revolving door issues, and we get that sorted and go straight into a cost of living crisis. Interest rates have gone from one-and-a-bit percent to four or five percent and it's all in a big melting pot.

So when we talk about KYC, if you've got the practitioner saying we should do remuneration planning, they've got three pivot points to work with. The Basic Rate band, the £100,000 rate band, (which is about not losing your personal allowances), or the additional rate band. If you don't know anything about your client, and what they need from a fiscal point of view, how can you do remuneration planning?

To me, it's as important. Knowing your client means you need to know that inflation has actually eroded away the personal rate bands. People's outgoings have probably increased more than 15-20 per cent plus over the last couple of years. Tax rates and corporation tax have gone up. You get this buzz because you want to help people who are going to struggle financially. If you sit there as an accountant and say, I'm going to give you remuneration advice, I'm going to give advice in the next two months before this tax year is up, and you haven't asked how much money the client wants. I think that's appalling."

> **Will to learn – remaining a leading-edge human firm**
> I enjoy the fact that Farnell Clarke has always been an early adopter of quality tech, and that it continues to improve on the thoughtful, quality services and insights for our clients. I'm happy that the drive to provide great services to clients enables us to spot efficiencies and stimuli such as VAT-MTD and KYC to help us implement and provide value added services for our clients and engaging ways of working for our staff. But for me, the biggest reason we need to adopt new business models to support our strategy to remain a leading-edge human firm is that it's what our clients want!

James Ashford on Know Your Client

"KYC is a critical compliance element within a firm and it's imperative this is understood and implemented as an ongoing process. It's also key that this is understood and capability is pushed right across the team, because you have many different levels of staff dealing with clients on an ongoing basis, and so they're the ones with the information. This is why any system you implement around KYC, must be a firm-wide system rather than sitting in the hands of the few, who may be disconnected from the facts.

But beyond this, you need to REALLY know your clients. If you don't know that they're planning to sell their business, or that their goal is to take their kids to school each day or that they want to buy a house abroad, then you don't really know your client. Do you know about their family? Do you know their hopes and dreams and fears?

Without this knowledge, there's no way you can be providing them with all the value you possibly can."

The take-home

- Any regulatory or legislative change can be used both as an excuse to clients and bootstrap method of accelerating the firm's transition to fully human. This is as true for systems and process changes as it is to find new ways get to know the client better or to establish deeper, more regular touchpoints,

- While KYC is necessary for compliance, it also provides an opportunity for firms to understand their clients' goals and support them in achieving their objectives,

- By collecting and analysing additional information through KYC, firms can offer tailored services and chargeable insights. They can also deepen the human bond through encouragement, understanding and empathy.

Notes

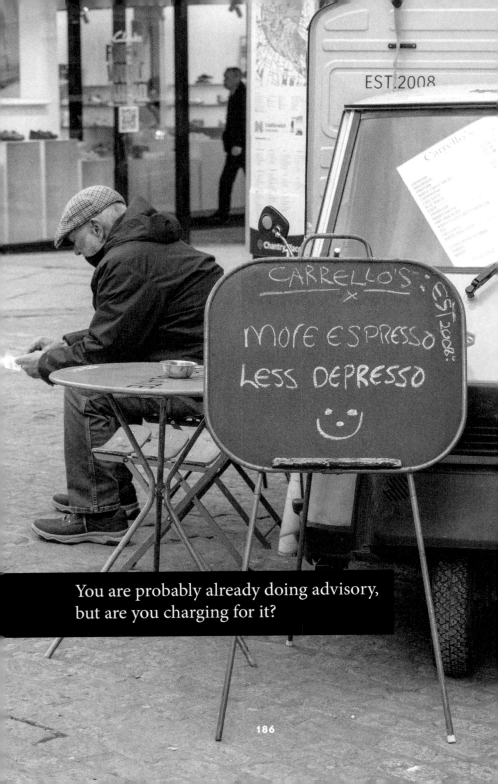

You are probably already doing advisory, but are you charging for it?

18

Insights and Advisory

THEN

"Do it smarter, more efficiently and provide more focused advisory to the client."

NOW

"With good quality timely data and consciously caring touchpoints we can really help our clients. And that's what we're here to do!"

There is no route map. No simple way to transform to a truly human-centric firm. It would be wrong for me to say that, and disingenuous. It might sound vague, but you're probably already doing advisory, and if you don't see it as a separate offering you're probably not charging for it. That needs to change and it won't harm you, promise.

Whether you are digitising your firm, humanising your firm, or making a decision on whether you want to be a compliance business, a compliance-plus business or an all-out advisory business, your next steps and your overall plan will be different. Each decision, ultimately, is down to you and the way you want to structure your firm.

Advisory can be anything from simple questions to detailed and rigorous analysis. In a round table I hosted at Sage Manchester, I asked the group for their view and each participant had a different take;

- Something relevant,
- Something the client can make a decision based on,

- Narrative from reporting tools doesn't cut it. Advisory is the software in our heads,

- Cash management advice, so the client can see what is spent, what is forecast, where additional funding is needed,

- Our clients come into the office and say, "I think I need to take on a new member of staff, can I afford them?" or, "Shall I have a new office or shall I buy hot desks?"

- It depends on the client. How much can they take out in the most tax efficient way, is only the start of it,

- Tech to help them,

- Good advice based on real time data,

- Anything that comes up in a conversation, or even starts one,

- It's about asking quality questions, if you could give them an immediate answer the clients could get there themselves,

- Taking them back to basics. How much do you want to earn, what's your sales price? What can you fit in? What based on that can you charge? And then working on that,

- As a business owner I am constantly paranoid. Is it all going to go wrong? So I expect my clients to need me to show them it's going to be OK,

- Our role is changing. As accountants we're like satnav in a car. We can help clients see the blind spots in their business and work with other specialists to help them.

A different level of insight –
Conversation with Alastair Barlow,
CEO and Co-Founder, flinder

I asked Alastair recently what client insight means to him.

"For me, it's having an informed opinion that you can take to clients in their sector on what good looks like, and have experiences from competitors, and fully understand the sector and their business or businesses, and it's about more than just financial facts. It's about looking at finance and non-financial data and actually understanding what it means, and what the implications are. And it's about making recommendations from that for tomorrow, to make life better for business owners and entrepreneurs.

To bring that to life, a simple example would be, it's not about saying what your gross profit was this month versus last month. It's about understanding that if you segment things down you can get useful actionable insights. Your customer acquisition costs in one territory might be higher than your customer acquisition costs in a different territory, right? Let's say acquisition costs in the US might be higher than your customer acquisition costs in the UK. On the face of it, you might go, "well, actually, our sales are about the same, so I'll stick to the UK". But actually, if you know and understand that US customers in a particular kind of segment are going to be longer standing customers, those customer acquisition cost might cost you more today, but with a longer client lifetime value you're going get more back. Therefore your LTV:CAC ratio is going to be much better, even if your payback period is less.

Having conversations like that is much more powerful than just going,"oh, this customer is more expensive, let's quit them," or even, "your gross profit this month is less than that last month, do you know why?" I don't think it's helpful to do that. I think it's helpful not to sit on the opposite side of the table, but on the same side of the table as the client, and work together. Not for one another, but with one another, and come to the right answers together, and have those kind of insightful discussions."

Good insight = good data

If we ask 100 accounting firms what does client insight mean, 90 per cent of them will say something far more simplistic, even though it's what they're striving for. It's so hard to convince people they can't even start to think about insight without good quality data. It's a different level.

Data is the first step. Another step is that you need to understand what your clients' business does. Yes, that's expected. But so many firms don't truly understand what their clients do. They don't understand how the clients revenue models work. We see it when we pick up new clients and review the previous firm's Xero data. You then need to actually realign the data taxonomy in the Chart of Accounts to see what that business does, and also to see how you should be managing performance. So you need access to all the other systems within the business that don't house finance information, the ones that house the rich why-it-has-happened information. This data offers a human connection.

Understand why it has happened from the non-finance systems, technology conversations, in the CRM system, in a Shopify system, understanding the business, understanding what the strategy is, and bringing that all together. Then you can have a much more insightful discussion, at Board level with clients.

From this you can see that client insights are limited only by your client, your data and your imagination, whether insights to clients through an entire outsourced finance function, benchmarking insights based on sectoral knowledge and expertise, App advisory services or personal finance management to high net worth clients, the sky is the limit.

Throughout this book I have identified key areas and ways that you might think through as you consider the best ways you can help your clients. In so doing I've emphasised the fact that you can only really do this is by understanding what it is they are striving to do.

To a point, then, the advice that you can take from this book largely depends on what you are trying to achieve, both for your accounting or bookkeeping firm, for your clients' business, or for your own life in general. What I've tried to do in this book is help you think through how insights and advisory might work for you, to decide how to structure your firm to support this, and to encourage you to think about the opportunities you might take and the direction you travel in.

In my view, and as far as Farnell Clarke is concerned, we know we are doing advisory properly when every client picks up the phone if they have an idea or a query. It's too easy for advisory to be pigeon-holed, when what it should be is the result of building the most robust, strong, open and enduring relationship with your clients, so that they can come to you when they want. That's what we are striving to do. We are building the most robust relationship we can with them so that we naturally become their go-to person when there's something they don't understand or want to talk through.

Driving insights

Helen Cockle told me she doesn't believe that what small business owners want has changed, because people don't know what they don't know. It's the role of the advisor to educate, and to date they have variable success. Helen believes that business owners often think they're on their own, and while advisors want to educate them, the disconnect between firm and client can be a challenge. Once, she says, the accuracy of data was always in question. Now it's possible to get the good quality, timely data that we need. To make sure that the data is coming in right so that firms' clients can truly utilise tech so that they spend their time proving real value is what it's all about.

To begin with it can feel like an uphill battle. David Lawrence recently wrote, "We know we do a great job, however, as the client doesn't see all the work going on in the background we have to find ways of showing clients our value". What can help, is in remembering that insights work in two ways, since the best way to help our clients is to have experience of the things we're advising on ourselves. A recent conversation with Eriona Bajrakurtaj revealed one way that this worked for her;

"We use GoProposal extensively! It has been a game changer for a number of reasons:

- Our clients cannot dispute our agreement to provide a service
- The price is clear from the outset,
- Engagement letters are automatically produced so I don't have to edit or write them each time (which was so annoying and time consuming),
- The dashboard is great for planning,
- Our pricing is so much clearer and more structured, so we are charging clients way more than we used to, and we can see where we were losing out,
- The results look super professional and impressive to our clients.

In essence, it has highlighted who we want to work with and who we do not!"

There are many routes towards potential advisory, new business and service lines. A chat with James Lizar about what the next five years might look like within the accounting and bookkeeping world around ESG illustrates this point well.

"Right now I think there are less than 10 certified BCorp accounting firms, I think we were number two or three, and we certified December '21. There are a few more in the pipeline already that I know of.

It's one thing to do if you are a business, but as an accountant we've got these spheres of influence. They are so powerful that if we can lead by example, we can get these other businesses to think, "hang on a minute. Maybe I've got permission to do that as well. I'm a bit scared of these spreadsheets in these numbers, but if my accountant is doing that, then maybe I can do that too." And we're certainly seeing that in our client base. We have seen businesses start to shift on the journey, not through direct conversations, just curiosity."

This made me wonder if there was a potential new service line offering, so I asked . . .

"Potentially. I've only just recently measured our carbon footprint. A year ago it was a nightmare. You'd go to the Carbon Trust website, download a spreadsheet, fill it in and find it's the same spreadsheet as the 500 person factory down the road. It made no sense. But very recently the tools have started to come on stream. Things like Spheric Stage Earth and Ecology Zero just started their launch. So the measurement tools for small businesses are starting to come in. I always thought this was the year that that would happen.

They are very basic at the moment, which is fine. I think this is one of the big adjustments we need to make over the next five years is that we are so accustomed to being able to get the truth to the penny – literally to the penny – because that's what the bank account says, and that bank account kind of drives all of the rest of it. With measuring carbon footprint it's different.

Will: We've got to accept that it's doesn't have to be right to the to the milligram.

James: Yes. And that's fine, because it's all about the comparisons like, how are we versus others. If your assumptions and errors are the same, then your comparative is going to hold, as you see, where you are making improvements, and see where the low hanging fruit is.

The next five years will I think be a pretty fast transition for a lot of businesses, and therefore accountants. It's potentially going to be quite a weird time. There will be a lot of regulation coming in and in place for big business.

If you're in a B2B supply chain, you are likely already pledged to net zero, because the person at the top has pledged it. I think the majority of the footsie 250 is pledged to net zero, and lots of banks have also pledged to change their investment profile, so that they are on a net zero journey (the one and a half percent version, so pretty aggressive). And so if you're on an RFP or you are on a tender for a big business, if you're applying to be on a preferred supplier list, if you're applying for a line, you're going to start seeing questions about your Net 0 credentials, which is going to be a bit of surprise. That's out there already, it's happening. And right now it's quite soft, like; 'do you have a one page Sustainability policy or not?' so you can quickly download one from google.

But this big business transition will start figuring in audit opinion as well. If a business is including a statement on their ESG credentials, then an audit firm is going to have to say whether it"s true and fair.

It will start impacting smaller businesses fairly rapidly. There are a lot of small businesses. So, right now it's an opportunity. Five years from now it's a threat."

The take-home

- You're probably already doing advisory, but you need to see it as a separate offering,
- The deeper and more authentic your communications with clients, the more likely your advisory services, (and therefore your revenue), will grow.

PART FIVE

MAKING
IT WORK

This section looks at how to navigate the practical and philosophical barriers to implementing successful change and covers aspects on establishing effective, efficient fully digital accounting since this is a necessary first step in the transition to The Human Firm.

Firms changed for the
pandemic, but what's
happening now?

19

Digital to Human, Why a Flick of a Switch isn't Enough

It's all about the people

As a business we have two choices – do we change or not. Do we have the desire, impetus and momentum to do this? Or not. It's that simple.

I've said it before and I'll say it again. Firms were able to change quickly – really quickly – when they had to because of the pandemic. If that was a strategic business decision by a multi-partner firm, for anything else, to even get to the point of agreeing a strategic change would be as part of what might be a five year cycle, (and would definitely not be days or weeks). But they did it in a week. All the hurdles to do something of that magnitude were navigated in less than a week. Decisions that would otherwise have been taken in 10 to 12 months were turned around in a matter of days. That proves it's all about attitude, about wanting to make a change happen.

Nearly every firm faces a challenge of 'failure to implement'. New processes, tech, client solutions, communications, team development, HR, marketing and more. This is not just a firm challenge, it's a challenge for all suppliers, vendors and consultants who seek to help the profession too. If you are going to make change, then you need to make sure it happens. In my experience it doesn't happen, (or doesn't happen usefully or doesn't stick), because it is not given the right focus.

> **"**
>
> *Everyone in a firm cares about the client. It's built into our accountants' DNA.*
>
> **"**

Everyone in a firm cares about the client. It's built into our accountants' DNA. So to get buy in we need to frame any change on the benefit to the client, whether this is direct or indirect. That will get the buy in you need from your management and wider team, which will help the prioritisation which will lead to project success.

And it is a project. Not operations. Something that has new systems, new processes, if you don't treat it as a project, (something with a finite end date and specific budget), and if you don't dedicate the resource to it you'll see the problem as time even though it isn't.

> **"**
>
> *If a change is to the client's benefit, that should drive the firm's behaviours, help us make and embed the change and should be run as a project. If it isn't to the client's benefit, why bother?*
>
> **"**

To get people to adopt and embed the change needs a similar approach to getting buy-in. That's why the focus on the client is so important. If everyone cares about the client and understands were not changing for the sake of it, but to make sure it's for the client, and if we're open about the challenges we experience, that should help embed the change, not hinder it.

Failure to implement, is it really about time and fear?

Regardless of your sector or sectors, failure to implement is a huge known risk. The components – less explicitly mentioned, especially in our sector – are acknowledged less often. Failure to implement may be a failure to implement new processes, to try new ways of working, to implement a new marketing strategy. Ultimately they're about a failure to change. As businesses we simply do not achieve our fullest potential unless we constantly evolve what we do to meet both internal and external drivers for change.

While speaking at a recent conference we took a straw poll of the audience. The single biggest reason for failure to implement was given as 'time'. Other reasons included fear of change, lack of the skills needed to change, information overload and 'if it ain't broke don't fix it'. Of course there are more, but they often have the same underlying reasons. Using the given reasons 'time' and 'fear' I'm going to explain what I mean.

Time

We will never have enough time. The underlying issue for failure to implement is not a lack of time, but rather one of prioritisation. OK, it's more complex than that. We firstly must prioritise the time to deliver the change we want. We need to treat any change as a project. Each change needs the necessary budget and resource. If it's a big enough priority with the right project management, you will successfully complete the project, implement the change and it will be embedded. If it's not a big priority? Whatever else you do to try to complete it isn't likely to be enough.

Fear

Change is never easy. However, in the Covid pandemic we all made the changes we needed. Look at how many businesses went from 100 per cent office-based working to 100 per cent remote in the space of a handful of days. Proof – should we need it – that when the driver for change is strong enough, we can do whatever we want. If this on its own doesn't work for you, turn fear of change on its head. Think about the consequences if you don't change. They'll most likely be worse.

Don't confuse change with operations, because this change is a project

You'd think it's a no-brainer, but sadly it's not. Any change is a project. Firms confuse daily operations, (which you know all about), with projects for a number of reasons; lack of definition, (daily operations are ongoing tasks and processes while projects re temporary endeavours with a specific goal and – hopefully – timeline), overlap, (daily operations may contain elements of projects and visa versa, something particularly true for process improvements), limited resources, (back to my point about prioritisation, don't make the mistake of believing that treating projects as daily operations will help you with resources), lack of planning, (failure to plan means it's easier for the change to get subsumed back into daily operations or deprioritised), and a short term focus, (and the 'it ain't broke don't fix it' cop-out).

From investigating the current tech stack and how things are done to planning how to integrate and train staff on planned changes, each task, action or development is a piece of a chain. It all requires project planning. Indeed, the old saying is true; failure to plan is like planning to fail.

The methodological take

We know that change management – what you are doing as you change your firm from Old-Style through Digital to Human – is more than project management, more than adopting and implementing new processes and technologies and more than communicating change. It is about considering the impact on human beings of the change and ensuring that employees and clients are both fully engaged and central to it. It doesn't come easily, but is necessary, nonetheless. It drives the successful adoption and use of change within a business, allows employees to understand and commit to the shift in process, practice and approach and to work effectively during the transition.

While the slavish following of one methodology framework or another is not – in my opinion – necessary or appropriate, here are some formal approaches that you could structure your thinking around. I've always preferred the first.

LEWIN's model, (which I've always preferred), has three stages; unfreeze the current state, move to a new state, and refreeze the new state. It emphasises the importance of understanding the current state and the forces driving change, as well as creating a plan for embedding the change into the organisation which – of course – involves communications.

ADKAR proposes five stages of change; Awareness, Desire, Knowledge, Ability and Reinforcement. It is big on the importance of individuals changing, the role of communication, education and of course reinforcement of change principles.

KOTTER's change model has eight steps; create urgency, put a team together, develop vision and strategies, communicate the changed vision, remove obstacles, set short-term goals, keep the momentum and make change stick. It emphasises the importance of communication, leadership and involvement of stakeholders in the change process.

The project centric take

1. A successful project requires a clearly defined scope, a known time frame, (with end date) and clearly defined roles. Manage this by explicitly defining the project with sufficient detail. Find ways to measure your goals so that you understand the extent of your progress.

2. Not understanding the 'why' behind the 'what' results in outcomes that don't meet peoples' expectations or the real organisational needs. Manage this by asking yourself 'why' to trace all the real requirements back to the basics. Poorly communicated project vision will result in poorly understood, (or non-existent), business benefits.

3. Prevent scope creep and project direction changes. This is more likely to occur when the project isn't well defined or planned, and can be managed with good change control.

4. Use the project vision and goals to aid decision making during project development.

5. Clearly define the start and end date, validate whether this is realistic and check your actual progress back to what is planned and understand any impacts. Monitoring progress, budget and achievements so that divergences from the project plan can be corrected early.

6. Define each project member's role, their dependencies on others and realistic time spans within which they can undertake their role.

7. Understand the business impact of the project on project' members time. Do they have time for your project and their other jobs? Make clear their priorities in advance if they are likely to have competing demands. Understand that context switching has a disproportionate effect on productivity.

8. Set up a route map so that you understand your critical path along with other tasks.

9. Define resources consistently (agendas, meetings, responsibilities, human, intellectual, financial structural resources etc) so that they don't jeopardise the project. Estimate as accurately as possibly, ideally using people who are familiar with the work required.

10. Start with realistic due dates. Allow extra time for unexpected events. They will happen.

11. Manage your stakeholders well. Identify principal stakeholders and ensure you have their input since without it your solution might not meet their expectations or needs ,(this includes your key clients). This is likely to prevent unrealistic expectations.

12. Great communication means great team and project management. Choose the right tools and processes to allow interaction between team members from the beginning.

13. Maintain transparency. Make sure everyone involved has complete visibility. This includes clear communications, good documentation and process management, transparency about tasks' statuses.

14. Manage risks as part of the project. This means considering them regularly and working out what might be done. One of the most effective ways to increase your project's likelihood of success is to do this and reduce potential issues from the start. No cop-outs here, you need a targeted (and not generic) risk log

15. Lead effectively, across all levels of a project in a robust and engaged manner.

The common sense take

While this is part of project management, it's worth considering separately. You can't succeed if you don't know where you're going. That means knowing the aspirations of existing and potential staff, existing and future clients and that of your firm. And by knowing I mean explicitly stating them and working out how you can manage the approach to success or to failure.

Will to learn – scope creep sorted

Just as with us, scope creep got Stefan Barrett as he grew Bee Motion. His solution was to get everyone to fill in timesheets and have a working file so he can cross reference work done with hours. This means he can identify variance as soon as possible. For more on our conversation check out the appendix.

Other ways to keep humans at the centre of change

1. **Engagement:** Foster an environment that encourages open communication and regular feedback sessions with employees, clients and contractors.

2. **Feedback:** Collect feedback from clients, client facing staff and other staff to gain insights into client needs and expectations.

3. **Transparency:** Yes, this is communication too, but important enough to be made explicit. Ensure regular updates and transparency with both clients and employees about the changes and how they may impact them and how they will benefit.

4. **Training and Development:** Provide training and development opportunities to employees to help them adapt to new technologies and processes.

5. **Culture and Values:** Clearly communicate the company's culture and values, and make sure that they align with the goals and objectives of the radical change. You'll find more on this in Chapter 15.

6. **Empowerment:** Empower employees to take ownership of their work and have a say in decision making processes. Ensure that clients know they're empowered to give feedback as to what they think as well.

7. **Technology Adoption:** Ensure that technology adoption is human-centred and meets the needs and preferences of employees and clients. Yes. Again it's important enough to be made explicit.

8. **Flexibility:** Offer flexible working options to employees and consider the impact of changes on their work-life balance, while making sure you retain the good things about team work and co-location.

9. **Collaboration and Teamwork:** Encourage collaboration and teamwork to promote a positive work culture and foster relationships between employees and clients. In times of change these things can get lost, but if you're not already doing this, your firm is unlikely to be sustainable.

10. **Recognition and Rewards:** Recognise and reward employees for their contributions and accomplishments to boost morale and motivation, and do the same for clients when appropriate.

Putting it together

To build a firm that is human inside and out needs a consideration, prioritisation and focus. Build the right team structures, understand internal and external touchpoints. You need buy-in, (and ideally understanding), from the principal stakeholders in your firm from the start, and you need to communicate clearly what is happening with your clients so that they understand it's for the best.

As you'd expect with something involving people, you need to understand where you're going, where you're coming from and the likely barriers to acceptance. You need to build an organisation that's attractive to the type of staff and clients you want, and be careful to communicate while you're doing so. You need to understand individual apps, app stacks, APIs and processes within each of these contexts and you need to understand that it will always, without exception, take longer than you think.

The take-home

Sometimes, the difference between success and failure is simply a result of being really clear on what we're trying to achieve. If a change is to the client's benefit, that should drive the firm's behaviours help us make and embed the change and should be run as a project. If it isn't to the client's benefit, why bother?

Making processes
that support your
purpose and priorities

206

20

Consider your Processes

THEN

"Automate the client's bookkeeping for them and you're no longer dependent on the client completing their data entry, (and associated accuracy challenges), plus you get the benefits of planning your workflow better. Take it one step further, and you can be working with and communicating with the client all year round."

NOW

"If you honestly put your client first this is no longer a choice."

One basic Really Big Thing

It's kind of basic, but before we even get to advisory, simply to be able to tell the client they can log into a cloud accounting tool and look at who owes them money, and that what they see is accurate 90 per cent of the time is a Really Big Thing. Like making the data current and reliable for clients. It is something that wouldn't have been possible ten years ago. If helping the client is where you're at, it's kind of mandatory now.

A financial controller or book keeper in an organisation would either enter bookkeeping data every day or insist that someone else did it, to ensure that all reporting was current. Why then, when providing the same reports as a paid-for outsourced service, do you think it's OK to provide information to your client once a month or once a quarter? Old-style accountants, dependent on data provided by a client carrier bag of receipts and a folder of invoices will never have current data. That matters.

To do any of this you need to consider your processes. Not the apps themselves, which I hope would be a given, but how they join and support your purpose and priorities.

Making post-Covid adjustments

If you made a transition to fully digital during the pandemic when you had to, you had to do it very quickly. As with all rushed things, there's a risk that the process wasn't fully thought through. How do you manage productivity? How do you measure progress, or for that matter anything else? How do you make sure our teams aren't missing out on valuable learning processes? Have you tweaked your processes since the transition? Are you making sure you're bringing people back into the office in the right way? Are you making sure that the right people are together in the right office at the right time? Are you sure that your processes help you identify and deliver client value?

Effectiveness, efficiency and support

Making sure that both tech and processes are in place to do things effectively is very important. Tech is often designed to be used in a particular way. It's not that you can't continue your old processes with any new tech you have introduced to your practice, but more like sticking to that old-new combination will be less efficient than what you were doing before.

Getting the balance of in-premises, (in-prem), and working-from-home, (wfh), time right is important in this new post-Covid era. It's important because your firm needs to support your people as authentically and efficiently as possible. It's important because you want to make sure that your firm is an attractive place for people to work, and it's important because your supporting processes should support both the business processes and the balancing act itself.

> **"**
>
> *Don't let the tech determine your outcome, because knee jerk adoption of tech will inevitably fail.*
>
> **"**

Most accounting firms can use cloud-based apps. They do it in bits and pieces. But they're not doing more than that. Flicking a switch to move operations from local to cloud-based operations is insufficient when the old-style processes remain. In The Digital Firm I wrote that manual accounting operations take double the time than those using technology. It's true, but not if you're using tech alongside your old manual processes. The key to success therefore is to start from the outcome. Decide on the best blend of people, processes and technology for your clients and your firm. Understand the benefits of bringing people in-prem and of letting them wfh. Whether tech or process, if a change has no direct or indirect benefit to the client, (whether through your efficiency or directly), you should understand what making a change will bring to your client, because if there is no client benefit you should not be doing it. Above all, don't let the tech determine your outcome, because knee jerk adoption of tech will inevitably fail.

While we go into it in more detail elsewhere in the book, good advisory is about being a good listener, about putting yourself in the client's shoes and about being able to ask – and respond to – the right questions. You can only do this with up-to-date quality data, which needs processes designed to support you and to help open the opportunity to see where you can help clients more. Processes supporting this will have a by-product of producing more revenue.

Even those who are bookkeeping or reporting on a quarterly basis haven't got it. The idea of getting your bank feeds direct into the software on a daily basis is to be able to turn that into meaningful data for your clients on a weekly or daily basis. Those who don't are missing the point.

Be more bullish

The importance of good quality timely data, as previously described.

If there is one fundamental mandatory and vital take-home from The Digital Firm it is that your data needs to be current. I said it in The Digital Firm. I'm still saying it today because – unbelievably – only five per cent of firms seem to have cottoned on. Seriously, the only way to have good quality current client data is to do-it-yourself. That means daily bookkeeping done in-house is no longer time consuming because of the bank feeds and apps that you can give to your clients.

As accountants, it's true, we have to educate our clients to make sure they photograph their receipts on a really regular basis, because there's no point in daily bookkeeping if your clients only send you their paperwork at the end of the month. For that reason, it's important to make sure the client understands the value to them. And in this respect whether you impose a single vendor on them or (as we do now) give them a (limited and managed) choice, the arguments are the same.

It's a no-brainer. I can't believe your clients will resist the idea unless they're picking up the resistance to change from you, or one of your staff. Who would say no to knowing their tax status or to knowing exactly who owed them money? However, since only a tiny percentage of firms appear to have brought all their clients into this way of operating, here's a list of arguments to help those clients still lagging make the change;

1. Real time data and greater transparency. If you can view your data in real time you can spot trends sooner, make better decisions, (faster), and get on top of creditors before they become a problem.

2. Faster processing. Recording transactions directly into an app is faster than doing it manually, faster than entering them into spreadsheets or ledgers and much faster than giving them to your accountant every so often. This can reduce your costs if you're using a bookkeeper and keep your accountants' bills predictable too. This is also true if you use apps for your invoicing, (which will enable faster processing).

3. Better cash-flow management and budgeting. You can budget and track income and expenses live, and with a good level of confidence of its accuracy which means you can manage your cash flow better.

4. Better security. An app has far more security features than that box of papers you're collecting.

5. Better customer service. You can respond to your customer enquiries faster and provide better customer service because the financial data is always up-to-date and available.

6. Cost effective. Fact! Apps are cheaper than bookkeepers.

7. Automatic categorisation. Most or your apps will automatically categorise your transactions, enabling you to track your expenses better and reducing the time taken, (and cost of), your accountant

8. Any time, anywhere, all at once. You will have better mobility since you can access your business information from anywhere

9. Reduced paperwork. Save the environment, reduce costs and reduce stress. No brainer!

10. Scalability. If you want to grow, this is the easiest way.

11. Reduced errors. By recording transactions directly into an app, you will minimise errors, ensure the accuracy of your financial records and reduce your accountant's costs.

12. Easier compliance. Apps don't just help you stay compliant with tax laws and regulations, they show the efforts you're making to do that.

I talked about the importance of good quality data, the time saved from systems-based reconciliations, the ways that regular data help with communications in The Digital Firm. I'll say it again, though. You have to have regular conversations with your clients, understand what keeps them up at night and daily bookkeeping facilitates this. Most firms still don't get it. So, just in case you need it for fellow partners or associates, here's a similar list for your practice, which of course considers both the client side apps and full cloud-based accounting;

1. Better decision making, strategic, (and even operational), advice and collaboration with clients because with real-time good-quality data the firm can provide better, more informed advice. That means more revenue.

2. Client satisfaction, (and therefore lifetime value), because of the improved, more seamless and efficient accounting experience they get.

3. Reduced Administrative burden, (if you're doing bookkeeping the old way).

4. Better, real-time data of good quality, (whether you are or are not).

5. Predictable, manageable bookkeeping costs at a predictable fraction of the old-style price.

6. More efficiency, less time, so better profits.

7. Increased ability to adapt quickly to regulatory and legislative requirements, (onus on the tech), and increased ability to identify value added services, (via better and more timely data).

8. Enhanced real-time reporting with client access to more timely information.

9. Better morale since client deadlines will be less stressful because of current data and plenty of time to refine and file.

10. Improved productivity through specially designed processing, automation of repetitive tasks, (including bookkeeping).

11. Better client relationships since a more responsible and proactive client relationship can be created.

12. Reduced costs when compared to local systems, distributed systems or office based manual processes.

13. Enhanced security through data encryption and secure data storage.

Will to learn – the fundamentals

The best way of explaining the true fundamentals, (and illustrating how far behind those firms are that don't do them), is to trace back how Farnell Clarke evolved. In 2008-9, the reason we were purely focused on an online GL was because there was nothing else. App ecosystem, App stacks – these weren't yet even concepts. At the time we used KashFlow as if we were using a desktop solution. We keyed in the data because that was all anyone could do. The benefits at the time were about 24/7 access to data, about being able to look at the same things that our clients were looking at, and that someone else would take care of the backup.

So if today people are doing the same thing, if they are saying "I've got all these clients. I want spreadsheets and I want my desktop and everyone's telling me we have to put them on the cloud, so I'm going to move them from Sage 50 to Sage Business Cloud Accounting so that I can tick the cloud box, haven't I done well!" The answer is NO! What they're saying there is what we did back in 2008-9.

AutoEntry didn't exist. Dext didn't exist. For me, the penny-drop moment came with ReceiptBank in 2011. I realised that no-one needed to put their receipts in an envelope any more because they could record them in an app on their phone. I realised this changed the whole game because we don't need to stay in the client's office to do their bookkeeping.

That's when we came to the fundamentals – the laggard's very basic minimum of cloud accounting. An integrated accounting tool to enable your clients to photo-record receipts so you don't have to do data entry.

The take-home

- Old-style accountants, dependent on data provided by a client carrier bag of receipts and a folder of invoices will never have current data. That matters. If you were working as a financial controller or book keeper in an organisation, you'd either be entering this information every day or insisting that someone else did it. Why, then, when providing the same reports as a paid service, do you think it's OK to provide information to your client once a month or once a quarter?

- It's kind of basic, but before we even get to advisory, simply to be able to tell the client they can log into a cloud accounting tool and look at who owes them money, and that what they see is accurate 90 per cent of the time is a Really Big Thing. Like making the data current and reliable for clients, It is something that wouldn't have been possible ten years ago. If helping the client is where you're at, it's kind of mandatory now,

- To do any of this you need to consider your processes. Not the apps themselves, which I hope would be a given, but how they join and support your purpose and priorities. So, firms that have done more than shift to tech need to have thought through the processes and matched them to the opportunities that the apps provide.

PART SIX

MAKING IT OUT

This section looks at the dangers of clinging blindly to one type of software, app, automation or processes and suggests ways of navigating the plethora of possible choices in the new accountancy app ecosystem.

Product parity,
firm parity and the
balance of control and
process efficiency

21

Tribalism and the New Landscape of Sharing

THEN

"In 2015 we decided that Xero was a better option for our client base at that time, and we migrated 600 clients from one platform to another."

NOW

"With greater product parity in a more mature market, as a business at FC we've developed scale that enables us to offer broader software choice whilst retaining the efficiency benefits previously available only from a single platform choice."

Community good, tribalism bad

When I set up Farnell Clarke in 2007, there was no way on this earth that another accounting firm would have sat down with me and shared their experience of what worked and what did not work. Nowadays there's a much greater openness, a much bigger sense of community and will to collaborate, along with this kind of new accounting business mindset where people accept that they don't have to treat everybody as competition. More than ever we can share our knowledge, capabilities, skillsets and opinions.

Farnell Clarke should probably have moved from KashFlow to Xero in 2013 but I had a deep emotional attachment to KashFlow as they played such a significant role in our development. Perhaps I was too blinkered, hanging on to the remote possibility that KashFlow might have caught up to Xero. That made it harder to make the switch when we did, because we had so many more clients. My tunnel vision could be considered a kind of tribalism that really wasn't there. There is a risk that those wedded entirely to a single platform, (especially now we have greater product parity), might not make the right tech choices for their clients. I wonder now if by delaying our migration to Xero that the systemic benefits we could have been unlocking for clients were perhaps also delayed.

The phrase 'economies of scale' suggests a financial impact, whereas in our case it was a resource benefit rather than money. Nowadays we are big enough to maintain the efficiencies in pods serving different platforms, but it's still about scale.

To see how tribalism might have developed with some core vendors, let's imagine what might have happened around Xero years ago. Perhaps they saw the apple app store and decided to build a similar sort of platform. Certainly around 2011-12 we saw Xero building proprietary tech that enabled apps to connect to Xero, from which emerged apps that grabbed tightly to this tech, (like GoCardless, Spotlight Reporting and ReceiptBank which then became Dext). These developers saw an opportunity to work closely with a market disrupter and as Xero grew, they grew too.

"

There's a challenge involved in balancing control in process with actually doing what's right for the client, particularly as we look to broader apps and usage.

"

Don't get me wrong, the core product, the one that sits at the heart of everything is important. But what happens if there is an add-on piece of tech that works better with a core product you don't use? How do you get that balance in terms of controlling process efficiency while actually recognising the needs of your client? There's a challenge involved in balancing control in process with actually doing what's right for the client, particularly as we look to broader apps and usage.

Back in The Digital Firm I was adamant that we had to stick to a single platform. This was largely because of the immaturity of the market and the difference between products that were market leaders. But competition meant that the distinctive characteristics of many core products are less evident now than they were five years ago.

The take-home

- There is now a greater sense of community and collaboration among accounting firms,

- Tribal attachment to a single platform can be either healthy or unhealthy, you need to review your decisions regularly,

- Balancing control and process efficiency with client needs can be quite a challenge,

- Market competition means the distinctive characteristics of many core products are less evident than they were five-years ago.

Separating sense from noise
in the busy app ecosystem

22

Too much noise

THEN

"We soon established that recognising data entry is something that will be automated is a big part of getting that new approach right."

NOW

"The idea came about to provide somewhere – one single, easy-to navigate place – that people can go and identify the apps that will do what they want."

As accountants we have an obligation to enable our clients to run the best business they can. Our tech works in a number of areas, and needs to do so, because we need to look at how we use the right apps and app stack to best support our clients and our own businesses. Blending the right people and process to meet our purpose is critical, both for us as accountants and our clients. If we don't help our clients, the risk is that our clients go to non-accountants to get their systems and tech advice.

There's another risk too. Clients are getting, well, not necessarily smarter, but more app-savvy. Millennials, GenZ, GenAlpha are all digital natives. If you don't understand how best to serve their dataflows, your clients may make their own decisions or – worse – you may lose them to someone that doesn't understand accounting data in which case your client won't get the efficiency they deserve. If this happens you may ultimately lose them because you can't meet expectations that were set up by that advice.

You know how amazingly low full digital adoption is around the world (I'd guess only five per cent of firms have really cracked the agenda, with a disproportionate number in Australia and New Zealand). Even now, very few firms are doing what I and my peers do with end-to-end digital. Many are trying. They're looking for the best choice for their clients and their own firms but things have got very much harder. In 2018 there were in the region of 600 relevant apps. Now there are multiple tools in well over 100 categories. There might be 20 pieces of tech in a financial reporting category alone. It's great in terms of choice, but we're seeing people succumb to app overwhelm because there is simply too much choice!

In one of Douglas Adams' books, his hero Dirk Gently becomes charmed by a device that could handle any calculation which returned an answer of anything up to four. Anything above four it represented as 'a suffusion of yellow.' The feelings he gets when his calculator gives this answer is – I think – as helpful as the plethora of app choices might feel to accountants when they want the best for their clients but don't quite know where to start.

Obligations app risk

The evolution of the Human Firm, a historical perspective

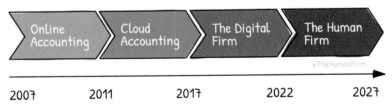

Will to Learn – reducing the noise

We had been using tech for a long time, were familiar with lots of tools and were fairly well known by app vendors and forward thinking firms alike. We were very fortunate in that we have a big address book. We know lots of firms and lots of vendors that we can call and ask questions. But back in 2019 we had an issue. We were taking on a new client and we were implementing some technology for them, (at the time, it was Xero, ReceiptBank and Workflow Max), but the client also needed purchase order approvals, so we looked at a product called ApprovalMax and had four pieces of technology that we were implementing as the core solution.

But when you are pulling four products together and want to design efficient workflows, the information isn't necessarily readily available since everybody is going to take different products as part of their mix. That was true for what we were doing, and we must have spent between eight and 10 hours in researching, calling people we knew, speaking to vendors to try and find out whether one thing integrates with the next, and if so how.

Later, in conversations with colleagues I said it's bizarre that we had to spend so much time doing this. Especially since the likelihood is that it would have taken somebody else twice as long. So the idea came about, to provide somewhere – one single, easy to navigate place – that people can go and identify the apps that will do what they want. So we decided to build App Advisory Plus, initially as a directory of apps and how they integrate, but also as a potential first line helpdesk, a knowledge platform and community for people to be able to share their ideas.

The point here is that we spent a lot of time on research and did not charge the client for it because we didn't have the mindset to do so, and because we didn't have the mindset we hadn't set up a process to follow that would ensure we saw it as a chargeable advisory service. Nowadays, we would manage expectations, ask what they are trying to achieve, what budget they had allowed and what outcomes they want. We would quote a price for going out and finding appropriate solutions and we would have recovered our time.

VUCA

VUCA is an overused acronym that stands for Volatility, Uncertainty, Complexity and Ambiguity. It describes a business environment characterised by rapid and unpredictable changes, high levels of uncertainty, intricate interdependencies and vague or incomplete information. I've heard it applied to the plethora of choice of apps and approaches in the accountancy app ecosystem. While I feel for the people who see things that way, and agree that there's a huge range of choice, too many variables, too few skilled staff, and a constant danger of overwhelm, I don't think the concept applies.

App overwhelm is real. Why – and how we resolved the challenge – is a Human Firm thing

The problem with cloud accounting and with software as services, is that the fundamental business model of app creators is different. New functionality doesn't drop in discs every six months or so like in the old days, but instead it's in sprints. And a sprint can be virtually any period, although they are often two-three weeks. That makes it nigh on impossible to keep up – or even be sure you're checking out the newest version! If you're a single person or even a small team you shouldn't be bothering.

If you just asked yourself how Farnell Clarke are making App Advisory Plus (AAP) work, you've not grasped the point of this book.

As a Human Firm, Farnell Clarke is all about our relationships. It's our job to make sure that relationships – between both vendors and accounting firms that use the platform – are there, are authentic and are current. That's how we're doing it, and what we are focusing on.

Of course there's more to it in terms of practicality and in how it supports our firm's purpose and strategy.

More on App Advisory Plus

When rolling out new tech, we have always used ourselves as the first guinea pigs. We then ask between five and a dozen digitally native clients if they'd trial it with us. We choose digital natives who weren't going to get upset if the platform didn't work right the first time.

If you are new to extending your app stack, or are looking to grow and add new tech, and if that tech has relevance to your own business. App Advisory Plus (AAP) is where you should start because we have built it to help you create your own white-labelled app advisory services for your clients. The platform is both directory and educational tool, with optional support services that we provide either directly or through the strategic consulting panel. We finally launched it at Accountex 2022. Although we first came up with and built AAP back in 2019 its official launch, like so many things, was postponed due to the pandemic.

AAP is still growing and covers over 450 accounting integrated apps across 40+ app categories and over 60 different business types. Registered users can build their own stacks of regularly recommended apps and even create white label reports, adding their own branding to share with their clients.

The site is completely free, includes educational and webinar content for end user firms and for the app developers to list and update their products and of course we're still improving it.

The good old 80-20 rule

Even if you take the larger app ecosystem, 80 per cent of the connections made to core GL products will be with 20 per cent of the solutions. Assume the same's true of accounting. Your pre-accounting and payment tools will be really high usage. They will probably account for a significant proportion of the total connections, and we're talking about tools that are connected to the core GL. 80 per cent of the tools connected to those GLs usually are only 20 per cent of the market. Our focus must therefore be on the most commonly used tools on our platform. For example while there might be 30 reporting apps, six or eight will be the most commonly used, with others important for niche areas. We will therefore concentrate on the former, and give everyone else the opportunity to keep their app details up to date, though we won't ignore the rest, because, for example tools that are relevant to verticals, (hospitality or project management type activities for example). Similar logic applies to consultancy, we need to focus on the tech and app stacks we're comfortable with advising on, and which we need to pull in external knowledge, such as inventory systems which can be much more complex to set up.

This means we can add functionality to help our individual human clients avoid the possibility of app overwhelm. Instead of having to start by examining the world of possible solutions, we will use our knowledge to help people funnel down to their best three solutions rather than a potential 30 or more.

Building an app advisory service line, advice for AAP clients

Four things you must do to minimise app overwhelm, (or one, if you want to keep life simple)

1. Identify your client's specific needs in terms of industry, features and functionality.

2. Look for integration capability. Choose apps that have a proven record of integration with other client apps, (or failing that your cloud GL), and offer smooth integration processes. Back this up by finding recommendations.

3. Consider the pricing including license fees, add-ons, maintenance costs.

4. Check reviews and ratings – comparisons from a variety of trusted platforms such as G2, Capterra and Trustpilot, (not facebook or LinkedIn unless you're really sure what you're asking, but a comparison of feedback from different platforms might compensate for perception bias).

Alternately, just use AAP!

AAP and App Advisory Explained

Our App Advisory Plus Service is a platform and optional consultancy service aimed at providing guidance to businesses that are looking to optimise their software usage. App Advisory is a service line firms can offer to their clients, while we've built the consultancy service for those who need help to do that.

We have suggested a structure within which App Advisory can be delivered, and if clients need it, it's how we would deliver it too. It is a five-unit process that involves a review of the business's processes, an assessment of the software requirements, and a recommendation of suitable software solutions. Each stage is optional, depending on the specific needs of the accountant.

During the initial review, a team of experts evaluates the business' current software usage and identifies areas where software can improve the efficiency of the business. The team also examines the business' goals and aspirations, to better understand how software can help achieve these objectives.

In the second step, the team assesses the business' software requirements, taking into account the current infrastructure, budget, and future needs. The team identifies suitable software solutions that will help the business achieve its goals and recommends the best options for them.

Finally, the team provides ongoing support and training to ensure that the chosen software is implemented and used effectively. This includes training on the features and functionality of the software, as well as ongoing support to troubleshoot any issues that may arise.

Overall, the App Advisory Plus Service is designed to help businesses improve their productivity and profitability by making the most of appropriate software applications. By providing guidance and support throughout the software implementation process, Farnell Clarke aims to help businesses achieve their full potential.

The take-home

- The fast changing nature of tech, and proliferation of apps can make it difficult for accountants to choose the right software for their clients. Choice is good, but too much choice can lead to analysis paralysis or poor decisions,

- Clients are becoming more app-savvy, particularly Millennials and younger generations, and may seek advice elsewhere if your firm can't meet their expectations,

- Full digital adoption is still relatively low among firms, with a large number of app choices leading to app overwhelm,

- App Advisory Plus was created as a single, easy-to-navigate directory of apps and as a potential helpdesk, knowledge platform and community for people to share ideas,

- Setting up a process to ensure that the client is charged for the time spent in investigation is a sensible advisory service,

- Understanding the client's goals, budget and desired outcomes is crucial,

- Technology can help optimise workflows and make client businesses more efficient, but requires expertise and guidance to be implemented.

Notes

PART SEVEN

MAKING IT COHERENT

Big picture and next steps

This section takes us back to the big picture, relates it to Client
Lifetime Value and reminds you that since you care deeply about
your client you should show it. It also contains conversations
which include insights and perspectives from a wide variety of
people in an even wider variety of firms.

Responsiveness to change,
future proofing,
Client Lifetime Value

23

Agile Visions: from Lifetime Value to Future Proofing

THEN

"Judging by what's happened over the last five years, the accounting market landscape will be unrecognisable in another five years' time."

NOW

"So little change. This is bonkers!"

Pattern, trend, future vision or horizon scanning. It doesn't matter what you call it, the tech results are clear. As tech products approach parity, such tech will not differentiate us at all. The processes we design to use these systems may be quite different because they will support the purpose, vision and values that differentiate us now. To leave my statement there would be disingenuous because what I've said doesn't explicitly discuss the most important thing. Our focus on the client, their needs and our mutual human interactions should be the driving factor. Not just for process development or for understanding how to maximise the value of every client touchpoint, but because staying human focused is the essential future proofing for everything that may come.

What can we do as service providers is bring our clients the right bits – whether the massive opportunity related to providing an outsourced finance function or something smaller, whether HR, wealth planning or any other service- at the right time. We can know our clients well enough to understand what they might be needing, and become accustomed to horizon scanning for trends and tech that helps prolong and deepen our relationships.

Firm agility, (including the firm's responsiveness to change, our ability to anticipate and benefit from new trends, disruptive approaches and low-margin market-seizing changes), must concentrate on deepening client relationships. The best future proofing, therefore is to extend our CLV and develop such good service options, deep relationships, an openness to queries and great personal communications that moving elsewhere is seen as unacceptable hassle.

It is a constant process, where we regularly look to the near and distant future, consider how clients might benefit and how we might extend CLV. Because as machine learning improves, as we get smarter artificial intelligence and as smarter RPAs do more of the number crunching we need to be clear on how we maintain our value as advisors. We need to start thinking now on what we need to do in terms of working out the kind of clients that we can make those impacts with and we need to reassess what we're doing and why we're doing things regularly over coming years, keeping both purpose and the human centric approach in our minds.

So technology might come along to do new things. MTD automation might – eventually – take a chunk from the bottom end of the market. To stay afloat then, or maintain sufficient value to pass on or sell more than minimal remaining goodwill in the future, everyone will have to move up the value chain. How do we position ourselves? What is our protectionist strategy around people that might be moving into the space that we're already in? How do we secure that part of our market? Is perhaps the larger premise to see our mix of skills and knowledge as a total-service provision in the same way that Enterprise Resource Planning (ERP) used to be the premise of larger firms?

A report from the Institute of the Future indicates 85 per cent of jobs that will exist by 2030 don't exist yet.

As long as you don't act like a robot – Conversation with John Toon

I had a long conversation with John about current and future visions. It was long, fascinating and exciting, and also for some firms terrifying, though he says;

"The good thing about being a human is that, as long as you don't act like a robot you can't be replaced by one." Here's his take on the future of robotic process automation.

"I guess the key thing is what do you define as RPA. First and foremost, because I think there are layers to RPA now. You will be familiar with products like Zapier, for example, or what used to be your Microsoft Flow which is an equivalent, and two or three of the general competitors out there. In general terms, that is RPA. It's relatively simplistic, only runs on clouds or Internet rooms and only runs with API enabled apps that you can connect to, but that's where the lines blur, with these low-code/no-code solutions.

And then while we talk about RPA as a solution like Microsoft Power Automate, which effectively replaces IFlow or Automation Anywhere. But where these solutions tend to dominate is when they also enable automation in an on-prem space, so in the desktop environment. And that's where there's a huge amount of power for both accountancy firms and for businesses. Again, it just depends on where you sit in the market.

If you're a cloud-first practice, products like Power Automate should be of little interest to you, because you should be able to connect things through API and have the data doing what you want and moving around between your systems as effectively as possible. Now you'll either do that with the built-in integration, or you'll use something like Zapier or you'll code it yourself or get developers to code it for you.

When it comes to a mid-sized firm like us, we're still in this hybrid environment, using on-prem solutions and cloud solutions. Things like RPA are hugely powerful for us, because they enable us to take essentially something that sits in a silo and an on-prem solution, and then connect it to a cloud solution, or vice versa, or create multiple connections between multiple environments.

Looking at the direction of travel for cloud solutions, for practice solutions, we should all be moving to the cloud. We know that CCH are moving that way. Iris is moving that way. Digita may or may not move that way as they're two or three years behind everyone else. But that's certainly the direction of travel and the direction of travel is to have open APIs. Between all of these things, I think that the purist view of where RPA can improve things, should in theory be relatively short-lived, because we shouldn't need to automate lots of things from the desktop for a long period of time, (let's say five to 10 years). That should be gone after then. But in terms of building up much more complex levels of automation, or doing things that the app developers and programmers are not going to build themselves, that is going to have a long, long tail effect.

The opportunities there are around all sorts of things. Every process in the practice, right from client on-boarding to disengagements, to billing, to the admin around sending out engagement letters. All of those things can be improved or facilitated with some kind of automation tool, although it doesn't have to necessarily be a robotic process automation. It could already be an automation that's built within a product itself, or it could be an integration between multiple products, where those integrations are already self built. They're automating a process. There's lots of opportunity there.

Where RPA becomes potentially even more interesting again, is when you start to think about what can you do with external data sources. Things like connecting to Companies House, for example, which obviously some products already do, connect to HMRC which again some products already do. To aggregate lots of data, you would have to use some kind of automation tool to manage and then cleanse that data. Then there's what you can do in terms of sending that out into an outward facing solution. Things like Companies House to get hold of benchmarking data so you can get hold of all the initial program load (IPL) data that's filed every month, and you could potentially benchmark lots of clients with that data.

Similarly we were able to report on stuff with one of our clients around the deprivation data for one clients' sites, and we could see how government incentives like free child care affect services in a particularly deprived area compared to a particularly affluent area, and indicate how many sessions were available as a consequence of governmental incentives.

Or, if you log into HMRC data, you could start to automate more of the processes around things like the tax return. You could have a chat bot on your website connected to HMRC and — let's say it was ChatGPT though it doesn't have to be — you could have secure processes in terms of verifying the person, their NI and UTR numbers, then have them upload information through a chatbot which could utlise RPA and an OCR extraction process to actually help complete a tax return. While the chatbot doesn't exist at the moment, I could have you coming on to our website, you could communicate with the chatbot which would ask you to upload things like your your tax statement, your p60 and things like that. We can extract all of that, because I already have something that works and does that for us at the moment in house. Then I could potentially have that file through tax software without anyone actually lifting a finger, other than checking the data extraction model and checking that the overall numbers are sort-of verified and checked."

THE HUMAN FIRM by WILL FARNELL

Exciting stuff, and a taste of the future, but whatever the future holds, tech poses a threat only if what you're doing is repetitive and doesn't need a human. The challenge will be keeping up, understanding how to stay human and making sure that every change we introduce into the firm will benefit the humans – the staff or the clients – directly or indirectly.

> **Low code and no code solutions**
> A low-code solution is most often used by tech professionals with some coding skills to create custom applications, while no-code platforms typically allow business users without any knowledge of coding to address their own development needs.

Never stop learning –
Conversation with Frances Kay, Director, Farnell Clarke

Pretty much all of a recent conversation with Frances showed our approach to continuous improvement and the learning that goes with it.

"We put in time sheets at the back end of last year. First we just tested it with a small group, then once we were comfortable we rolled it out. So long as there is a business case for making a change – something that benefits the client, directly or indirectly – then it's worthwhile embedding and looking at the remaining tasks.

At the moment, I'm doing a course on business systems automation. It blows my mind what really mundane things can be automated, or that you can get AI to tell you what to do. I would say we've still got quite a lot of routine tasks left that we can let the robots do. It's really exciting to see what can be achieved. Apparently ChatGPT almost passed an ACA exam. That's mental! Don't ask Google, just go straight to ChatGPT and ask that! It's quite fascinating to see how that will turn out in the future. I mean, you kind of think, oh, it's cheating, right? But actually it isn't. It's getting rid of that mundane work, and you can add the value on top."

This applies across the board, with communications too.

"Maintaining excellent communications. Providing great timely responses. That's something that can always be improved. It's like hunting for unicorns, not quite there yet. You can use so many tools. Emails, WhatsApp, OpenSpace for security, but if you ask a client a query – usually via email – they probably don't answer fully the first time. Then it goes back and forth. There are apps out there on the market but I'm just – well, that's another app. Clients are communicating with us at least four different ways already. Now if you have a query it needs to go to this app. I don't think that's the way to nail it. Maybe we don't have the right system in place, and it's going to change over time too."

No AI and a global workforce

"I think the interesting thing is that we chose not to use AI," said Helen Cockle to me recently. Futrli made the decision to build their own accounting algorithms because they needed to think like an accountant, not just look at trends of numbers. Their objective – to transform numbers into things that help their client accountancy partners to truly understand impacts on their clients' businesses – means that they had to think carefully about what they had to code. AI, she said, just isn't built to provide that level of complexity, not least because when there is data in small businesses it tends to be quite lumpy, and what can AI help you deliver when there's no taxonomy at all?

Meanwhile my conversation with Kenji Kuramoto of Acuity revealed that he's expecting the future to be more of the trends that we're seeing today; "Using the most powerful tools in our profession will create great opportunities for flexibility and growth. Those firms that are not fearful of the tech or of being replaced by it will continue to outpace others." Another trend he's expecting to increase is tapping into the global workforce. Flexibility will be as important as a strong firm personality.

The take-home

The constant, ongoing development of new ways to extend the CLV results in an agile firm, the best form of future-proofing.

- Regular horizon scanning is important, as we consider current and future trends, how clients might benefit and how to continue to do this as the accounting market landscape and tech that services it changes radically,

- The use of technology alone will not differentiate accountancy service providers, but rather the processes created to support purpose, vision and values,

- Staying human-focused is the essential future proofing for everything that may come, as the accounting market landscape changes, and this includes tapping into the global workforce with flexibility and while maintaining a strong firm personality,

- By considering a client's value over its entire lifetime with the firm (CLV) and how to deepen or extend that value, we can be sure of properly considering how best to serve the client.

Notes

The only certainty is change, but if you act like a robot you'll be replaced by one

242

24

In Conclusion

"As much as I appreciate the frictionless experience of digital platforms and the decentralised nature of the Blockchain, there's still a lot to like about old good centralised and physical institutions where you can just knock on the door, talk to a real person, and prove that you are you. Human to human. Not human to AI. Not avatar to avatar."

NICOLAS VAN ZEEBROEK, ULB SOLVAY

I started this chapter with a quote from a non-accountant because he said so well what is a universal truth. The spread and quality of apps supporting cloud accounting functions are converging. In the future they'll not provide us with key differentiators at all. AI, robots and machine automation are making such strides that it's hard to see what process-driven work might remain, and while it's possible to imagine a practice holding fast to some time-consuming, manual process, the differing time over which work could be done will price their work right out of the market.

What is left? Although the no-brainer digital adoption I wrote about in my earlier book still hasn't happened, there is one thing I can guarantee. What I can say, absolutely, is that the human side of accounting will be of overriding importance. While apps, AI, robotics, machine learning and tech can provide huge benefits to accounting firms and their clients, they are – at base – tools that require skilled professionals to use them effectively. Purpose. Communications. Relationships. Intuition. Perspective. Insight. Empathy. Imagination. These are the things we can bring to our clients in the fully Human Firm.

What is important when client experience is key? Everything!

Strive, work, think, communicate, make changes, check them and repeat, again. Farnell Clarke is striving to become an authentic, fully integrated, seamlessly human firm in the same way we cracked becoming a fully digital firm at the time I wrote my last book.

We're not there yet, but we're leaders. We have clarity of purpose and a huge focus on client experience. We've already articulated our value propositions to clients and employees alike. We're now deep in putting in place the collateral human processes, really focusing on quality lifetime value that we can deliver to our clients.

At the same time, and as a result of delivering a quality difference to our clients, we're making sure we've created the right career path for our team members. We know our firm's personality will continue to evolve as we mature. Through those things we aim to become the ultimate destination for people who want to work with a modern and innovative, forward-thinking accountancy firm.

We are making sure we're delivering true client insights through having a complete handle and control over the relevant data. We're thinking about the opportunities that data science gives us, since true analytics will lead us to better understanding.

The evolution of the Human Firm, a historical perspective

I urge you to think about these things. You care deeply about your clients, so show it. Make changes, develop to demonstrate it more. Think about your own firm, its purpose and where you are going. Look at the processes supporting properly good quality data. That's what we're doing. We're keeping tight focus to make sure we run the best, most profitable, most efficient and informative firm that we can. Only then can we really properly deliver for our clients.

If you haven't done it yet, think about making your purpose as clear as possible. Clarity of purpose will keep you on the right track. Faith in your purpose will drive your behaviour, your decisions, the way you behave with team and clients. Put that at the heart of everything you do in your own business. Use the experience to help clients think about the purpose, and work out how you can support them in delivering that purpose for themselves and in terms of their clients.

Get there ahead of the curve. Let other accounting practices wait for external catalysts to force a change upon them. It's not healthy to do so. Whether these catalysts are KYC, Son of MTD, as-yet-unanticipated low-end automation or new regulation, don't wait until you're driven into the move to Human. By the time those old-style accounting practices realise they're haemorrhaging clients it will most likely be too late to for them to pick themselves up.

Stay human, be original, focus on your clients. The rest – and your success – is up to you.

PART EIGHT

APPENDICES

We Want Your Feedback

Why I Chose Sage

Sage

Acknowledgements

About the Contributors

Conversations

Glossary

We Want
Your Feedback

Honestly, I wouldn't be me if I didn't want your feedback! Suggestions, improvements, omissions and what you think. On LinkedIn, Amazon, Audible, Kindle, Trustpilot – through the Sage website or through Farnell Clarke's website... wherever!

Here are some links you might like to use.

www.linkedin.com/in/willfarnell

www.linkedin.com/today/author/willfarnell/

www.linkedin.com/company/farnell-clarke-limited/

www.facebook.com/FarnellClarke/

www.sage.com/thehumanfirm

www.willfarnell.com

Why I Chose Sage

I have had the opportunity to inspire and influence firm owners from stages around the world for a number of years. My original purpose for Farnell Clarke – to change the way professional services were delivered and perceived by those that use them – has led me to want to help accountants and bookkeepers make the most of the opportunities around them, by perfectly blending people, process and technology.

For anyone on a mission like this, reach is critical!

I have had the pleasure of working with James Ashford and his GoProposal team for a number of years. For me, their fundamental success wasn't driven by overly selling their product, but by focussing on thought leadership, education and the betterment of the industry as a whole.

The Sage acquisition of GoProposal and then Futrli (who we also have long relationships with) created a light bulb moment, in seeing Sage publish James' second book – "Untapped."

Sage shares my passion to educate and support accountants and bookkeepers, to digitise and humanise what we do and to deliver world-class client experiences as a by-product.

Since writing "The Digital Firm" my thinking has developed further. Over the last five years, this developed into an embryonic idea of this book which I took to Sage, and then developed to this book; "The Human Firm"

I am hugely thankful to James, Neal and the team at Sage for having faith in me to write this book and to give me full artistic freedom to call it as I see it. I am excited by Sage's direction of travel. Its recent acquisitions show a genuine desire and commitment to providing the tools required by growth-minded firms to digitise and become truly client-centric.

Their willingness to back the education required to support this adoption and humanisation makes me hugely excited to help thousands of accountants and bookkeepers in the UK and around the world run better firms and in doing so, improve the lives of their clients.

Will Farnell

Sage

Sage for Accountants can help you build and scale a human firm, faster, by giving you the power to go from proposal to advisory within one platform. Use Sage for Accountants tools including GoProposal, AutoEntry and Futrli to elevate your work, maximise your client impact and run a more fulfilling and profitable practice.

GoProposal enables you to price consistently, sell more confidently and minimise risk with every client engagement through professional proposals, AML and automated engagement letters that can be sent, signed, and returned electronically.

AutoEntry removes the grind of manual data entry for invoices, receipts and bank statements. Scan, snap and upload on the go via email or with our mobile app or let AutoEntry automatically fetch them from online sources.

Futrli provides accountants with data-driven three-way forecast financials, using propriety prediction algorithms, giving them the power of advisory and enabling their customers to visualise the past, present, and future of their business.

To access exclusive resources and to go from proposal to advisory with the power of Sage for Accountants, visit: www.sage.com/thehumanfirm

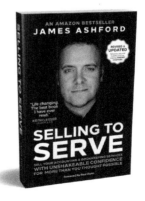

Acknowledgements

My first thanks for this book go to James Ashford and Neal Watkins. You see, this book has been alive in my head for some time, and James has listened to me grumble about the apparent lack of education from software vendors to help firms understand how to get real value from their technology. Our discussions lead James to get buy-in from Neal Watkins at Sage, through which Sage agreed to publish this book. Huge thanks therefore to the whole team at Sage who enabled us to get it out. James' involvement goes much deeper; through his encouragement, belief in the topic, and of course his hidden skills as an artist. He single-handedly designed the cover and produced the illustrations you'll have seen throughout The Human Firm.

Now, as I sit here and think about all the people that have played their part in this second book I simply can't ignore the thousands who took the time to read the first one, and whose feedback inspired me to write this. I still take immense pride when accountants, bookkeepers and vendors share with me the impact The Digital Firm had on their businesses. Thank you all.

Much of this book tells the Farnell Clarke story. To a degree, it's where we have been, but it's more about where we are trying to go. We're not there yet, not by any means. But I hope that, in charting our course, it will help others. Much of the first half of Farnell Clarke's history was directed through my view of the world. The second half has been shaped as much by my co-directors James and Frances Kay. Without them both, the business would be both different and probably smaller. More recently, our Non-Executive Director, Louise Kingston has brought a new dimension to our business, my own thinking and our working practices. Thank you, Louise, for that and a huge thanks to our team and clients, past and present. As a Human Firm both in terms of our aspirations and our constantly improving practices, we grow together, through mistakes and successes and appreciate you all the more for that. Thanks also to Farnell Clarke members Lauren Sanders who recently joined us as HR director for her input to the book and to Vince Burton who took the photos you see in the book at the start of each section and chapter.

I might have had the ideas, but delivery is made possible by a whole load of other people and the many partners we have had on the Farnell Clarke journey. Thanks to Carole Edrich who made all my ramblings logical and digestible, and without whom you would not be reading this book. And to her team; editor Jaime Breitnauer, subs Jane Zacharzewski, Lindsay Carstens and Simon Edrich, and designer Gavin Ives.

A number of people contributed time and great insight. Originally anticipated as mini case studies or quotes, the conversations were so informative, and showed the fundamental element of the book – human conversations and insight – that it felt wrong not to share our conversations in their entirety. Thank you for sharing your stories by doing so illustrating so well the things the book set out to deliver; Alastair Barlow, Chris Downing, Eriona Bajrakurtaj, Helen Cockle, James Lizars, John Toon, Karen Kennedy, Kenji Kuramoto, Maisie Poskitt, Richard Bertin, Rob Brown, Roger Miles, Sam Mitcham and Stefan Barrett. Thank you also for comments that were so good we had to include them; Brian Coventry, Dexter Lawrence, Eleanor Shakeshaft, Lisa Daniels, Luke Millar and Nicolas Van Zeebroek.

To kick off the project and test the thinking and theory, Sage hosted a round table. The people who were there got us thinking, and were used as foundations for some of the conversations. You'll have found some extracts from this through the book. Thank you for attending; Alexandra Macleod, Georgi Rollings, Glenn Martin, Hannah Adams, Helen Rogers, Ian Butler, Johnathan Mackie, Kamlesh Rajput, Matthew McConnell, Michael Braun, Neil Whittingham, Paul Barnes, Phil Ellerby, Rebecca Williams and Wesley Nunns.

Thanks also to the Beta Readers. Unfortunately I can't name you all here because this chapter's part of what you're reading. Your work is so very much appreciated. The more eyes on – and feedback about – this book before print the better it and the supporting assets will be.

Of course, none of this would have been possible without support from my family. Thank you to my wife Jill and to our parents. Your constant support is both important to me and so very appreciated. Thank you also to my children, who have become accustomed to my disappearing on and off, sometimes for days at a time.

There are far too many others to mention individually. Thank you for being part of this journey, whether we have had conversations, chats on LinkedIn, facebook or whatsapp, whether clients or staff, or suppliers … or anyone. You've helped shaped our business, our thinking and this book. I hope you enjoy it, let me know what you think and join in as we celebrate its completion. It's the end product of Farnell Clarke's development and of our thinking, for now…

About the Contributors

The following biographies are in order of their appearance.

Will Farnell
Owner: Farnell Clarke

I'm Will Farnell. I love helping accountants get excited about tech and what it can do to underpin growth. As the owner of the innovative and pioneering accountancy firm myself, I know first hand how it feels working to implement true change. I'm an entrepreneur who is passionate about giving great service and finding radical solutions to provide value and establish efficiencies.

I set up Farnell Clarke in 2007 with the sole objective of making accountancy simple and easy for clients. We're well on the way to doing this now, and my mission is to help other firm owners do the same.

I'm all about flexibility, about finding a good life-work balance, about finding the best approach of our accountancy and business advisory services for our clients and about empowering our staff. None of that would be possible had we not adopted the best tech available. I'm keen to share what I've learned along with our mistakes to help you find your next steps as you transition your firm through fully digital to The Human Firm.

When I set up Farnell Clarke in 2007 there was one objective, to make accountancy simple and easy for our clients. We are well on the way to doing this for our clients. These days my mission is to help other firm owners do the same for their clients through consulting, mentoring and speaking.

For more, see www.willfarnell.com/page/work-with-me

Sam Mitcham
Founder of SJCM Accountancy

Sam, an AAT licensed accountant, formed SJCM Accountancy in 2019 having spent 13 years employed in practice. SJCM Accountancy focus on balancing the use of modern technology with the importance of humanity. Sam thrives on helping small business owners better understand their numbers, be ahead of compliance and perform at their best. Sam also enjoys giving back to the accountancy profession and can often be found online, or on stage, sharing her personal experiences of running a business.

Helen Cockle
Chief Operating Officer, Futrli for Sage

Helen has entrepreneurialism in her veins. Prior to joining Futrli, she founded two thriving retail businesses, both of which she led to successful sale. With this experience under her belt, Helen is now proud to be at the forefront of global change in the small business economy. She is a huge advocate for equality and diversity in the workplace and believes the glass ceiling is there to be broken.

Chris Downing
Director of Product Management
for accountants and bookkeepers at Sage

Chris brings a wealth of strategic insight, empathy, hands-on experience, and the voice of the accountant into the heart of Sage, having spent the first 19 years of his career with the top 100 firm Milsted Langdon.

Kenji Kuramoto
Founder of Acuity

Kenji is the Founder and CEO of Acuity which builds and maintains financial functions for innovative entrepreneurs. Through Acuity, he's provided over two thousand companies with a full range of financial solutions from high-level strategic financial counsel through its fractional CFO practice all the way to virtualized bookkeeping and tax services. Acuity has been named one of Accounting Today's Top Firms For Technology and Top Firms To Work For. He is actively engaged in the accounting profession and has served on the advisory board for industry tech companies such as Gusto, Xero, Freshbooks, and Expensify. Kenji is also the co-founder of Acuity Invests which makes seed-level investments in Accounting Technology, SaaS, FinTech, and Crypto companies.

Rob Brown
Accounting Influencers Podcast

Rob Brown hosts the Accounting Influencers Podcast and is co-founder of Accounting Influencers Roundtable (AIR). He is a renowned presenter, facilitator and chair of high-level conferences, panels and events globally for the accounting and fintech profession. He is retained by many professional networks, alliances, associations, practices and vendors to chair their events and provide high-level interview content for their communities. He is a dynamic speaker and accomplished expert on trust, reputation, employer brand, talent, career development, succession, GenZ/generations, executive presence, referrals, networking and winning new business.

Maisie Poskitt
Head of Amazing at BHP LLP

Maisie is currently the Head of Amazing at BHP LLP. After working in practice for seven years, and gaining her AAT and ACA, she took a support role in her firm and is now charged with the induction of all staff and the review of training and software needs of the firm. During the following three years, she has championed the voices of GenZ's entering the workforce and challenged the industry's perception of the future accountant.

Stefan Barrett
Founder of Bee Motion

Stefan is an accomplished, passionate accountant and entrepreneur who founded Bee Motion in April 2015. He brings inclusivity to the forefront of the company's values, making sure that every client is catered to according to their unique needs. Stefan's commitment to perfection, attention to detail, and passion for helping businesses succeed have helped Bee Motion become a highly respected and sought-after accounting firm.

Stefan's experience with the Apprentice Academy has made him a strong advocate of their training regime. He actively recruits apprentices within Bee Motion with the goal of promoting growth and development for both the business and the apprentices. Stefan believes that as Bee Motion expands, apprentices should grow with the business and eventually fill senior positions. By nurturing and mentoring these apprentices, he also aims to ensure that the core culture and working ethos of the business are maintained and passed on to future leaders within Bee Motion.

This approach to talent development can help build a strong and sustainable talent pipeline for the firm, ensuring that it has the skills and expertise necessary to thrive in the long term.

Stefan likes to keep active and enjoys scuba diving, snowboarding and working towards his private pilots licence in his spare time.

Eriona Bajrakurtaj
Managing Director of Majors Accounts

Eriona has worked for Major's from a young age alongside her studies at world renowned educational institutions, she has transformed it to the cloud-practice it is today. She is also a member of the Quickbooks' Accountant Council, and works closely with the ACCA. In her spare time she is involved in property development, which is something of a passion. Eriona also has two 'beautiful' children who she tries to spend as much time with as possible. Eriona loves travelling with her family so her children can see the world and they can gain new experiences together.

James Kay
Managing Director, Farnell Clarke

James joined Farnell Clarke in 2016 as director and shareholder. Having worked within both financial and operational roles at a senior level, James' initial focus was to develop the structure and processes within the business to better manage the impressive growth that has continued to this day. James is now responsible for the overall strategy for Farnell Clarke moving forward, including the future plans for growth.

James Ashford
Founder of GoProposal for Sage

James Ashford is the founder of GoProposal, which enables accounting and bookkeeping businesses to price consistently, sell more confidently and minimise risk with every client engagement. He is the bestselling author of 'Selling to Serve' which teaches you how to sell your accounting & bookkeeping services with unshakeable confidence for more than you thought possible, and 'Untapped' which shows you how to break through the fear & grow your revenue from existing clients.

In 2021, Sage acquired GoProposal as part of their commitment to providing accounting businesses with industry leading tools, so they can build more efficient, insightful, profitable businesses themselves, and in turn, have a greater impact on their clients.

Lauren Sanders
HR Director, Farnell Clarke

Lauren has been working as the HR Director at Farnell Clarke since April 2022, helping them to get Great Place to Work accreditation for the first time in the company's history. With almost two decades of HR and organisation design experience, Lauren has worked across multiple sectors from manufacturing to healthcare, to bio tech and government.

Lauren is a member of the CIPD and also holds a Masters in Occupational Psychology and specialist interest in business resilience, socio-technical design, and organisation change. She currently oversees the people elements of Farnell Clarke's strategy and has also engaged a number of clients offering similar services to assist in their growth.

Having previously owned a furniture making business, she brings with her a lived experience of the pressures that business owners face and understanding of the need for support from the experts in HR and finance services.

Karen Kennedy
Founder of Kennedy Accountancy

Karen Kennedy set up Kennedy Accountancy in October 2020 during the Covid lockdown. Karen is based in Dornie and Kennedy Accountancy serves, first and foremost, the local business community in Lochalsh & Skye, with a focus on utilising technology as much as possible and helping clients run better businesses.

James Lizars
Founder Thrive Accountants

James Lizars is a member of ACCA's Global Council and the founder of Thrive Accountants in West Sussex, a Xero partner firm specialising in early-stage technology businesses.

As one of the first UK accounting businesses to achieve B Corp certification and as one of the early partners of the Million Tree Pledge initiative, Thrive has an established track record of demonstrating the business case for sustainability. They achieved recognition for this work in 2022 as winners of the International Accounting Bulletin's award for Sustainability initiative of the Year.

Richard Bertin
Founder and CEO of All In Place

Richard Bertin is a Chartered Accountant, former chair of various committees and current ICAEW Personal Financial Planning Advisory Group member. He established and built up a successful fee-based wealth planning business, selling a stake in 2016 to Stonehage Fleming, the largest independent family office in EMEA. Then he launched AllInOnePlace, a Fintech platform for the accountancy profession and having great fun doing it! Otherwise he's out on the motorbike.

Alastair Barlow
CEO and co-founder of flinder

Alastair is the CEO and co-founder of flinder, a business that builds and runs smart finance functions* and data analytics for fast-growth and complex businesses. Prior to founding flinder, Alastair spent 16 years at PwC in various roles across consulting and assurance. He is a qualified accountant, speaker, and judge and adviser to industry forums.

Alastair is passionate about the convergence of accountancy and data to deliver insight, which is the core foundation of flinder.

Outside of work he enjoys spending time with his daughter, fitness, cycling, snowboarding, skiing, reading, self-development, business, motorsports, rugby, international travel and the arts.

Frances Kay
Client Services Director, Farnell Clarke

Frances has been at Farnell Clarke since 2013 and became a director and shareholder in 2015. Frances is responsible for the continuous improvement of client experience and delivery processes, team development and business development for our London-based and larger clients. Frances' track record and strengths lie in harnessing contemporary technology solutions to systemise and streamline processes, delivering the best service in the most efficient, scalable and repeatable way.

John Toon
Senior Manager at Beever and Struthers

John is a qualified accountant who can add up but hates tax returns. He has a passion for the tech side and 'waffles on' about it Ad nauseam, usually on his podcast. John has a ridiculo Big Four alumnus usly encyclopaedic knowledge of the accounting and audit tech scene. Beware, he says he also has opinions and is willing to share them.

In his own words, he says he is 'disorganised, easily bored and not a fan of mundane tasks'. But give him a challenge or a problem to solve and he will smash it.

Conversations

The conversations I had with people in preparation for this book were so rich, so informative and so human that we agreed to share them with you online. Get a flavour with the summaries and extracts in this appendix and reach them in their entirety through the Human Firm landing page **www.sage.com/thehumanfirm**.

Conversation with Alastair Barlow

In this conversation we discuss the role of technology in accounting and the future of the profession.

Alastair begins by talking about how the role of an accountant has evolved from being purely technical to requiring a broad range of skills including commercial awareness,, data analysis and strong relationship and communications skills. He believes these are as necessary for accountancy as they are for emerging professions and that in the future accountants will have specialists in the areas.

I agree, and we talk about data storytellers which I don't believe AI will replace any time soon. We then discuss the tech in our own businesses, the building of a data analytics platform, and using AI tools such as Syntethsia for video recording and Tonic.ai for building demo data.

Alastair notes that a year ago he'd have thought that the use of AI was way off in the future, but now, with the release of ChatGPT and the potential for Google and ChatGPT4 he believes that augmenting human work with AI is closer than we think. He envisions a future where an AI system could answer basic questions about revenue or other financial metrics, but still sees a need for human accountants to provide insights and make connections. I agree, but note that since only around 5% of UK accounting firms currently provide daily data to clients, there's still a lot of room for improvement.

The evolution of the accounting and finance service model
© flinder, 2023

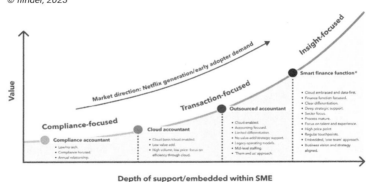

Conversation
with Chris Downing

In our conversation, we discuss the challenges and opportunities facing the accounting industry in the next five, 10, and 15 years.

Chris predicts that technology will continue to shape the industry and that accountants will need to adapt to remain competitive, and notes that an increasing demand for instant advice from clients might already lead to some feeling there's a conflict between providing value and getting paid for their services. We agree that accountants need to educate their clients about the value they bring beyond compliance, and find ways to find insights or collaborate with other experts to offer more specialised service lines.

The conversation then turns to the slow adoption of cloud-based technology in the accounting industry. Chris believes that both timing and having enough time are both crucial factors, as accountants can struggle to find the time themselves (through workload) and can also struggle to find the right time to introduce new technology to their clients. We agree that the lack of integration between data capture and bookkeeping is a barrier to adoption, and that accountants may need to be more proactive in making their work easier through using a seamless approach to technology.

Chris shares his experience around the importance of face-to-face interactions in driving adoption of technology, as not everyone is comfortable with digital communication channels.

Chris speculates that the VAT-registered businesses have already adopted OCR tools and other cloud-based technology, but the smaller, non-VAT registered businesses may need more convincing. He also talks about how the cost of software and other digital tools may be a barrier to adoption for smaller businesses, but accountants need to find ways to have the conversation about digitalisation and the potential benefits it can bring.

Conversation with Eriona Bajrakurtaj

Eriona starts by relating how she brought her firm from traditional manual processes to fully Cloud based just in time for the first lockdown, moves on to discussing the challenges in bringing staff through the digital transformation and then talks about the challenges of finding the right people post-pandemic.

At times our conversation diverts into the aspirations behind the conversion, how she is encouraging clients to choose more online face-to-face time over time consuming physical trips to the office, how her father bought into the benefits of Cloud-based apps and processes and her plans for the medium and longer term future.

Conversation with Frances Kay

This conversation, which is between Frances Kay – who I know and work with daily - and Carole Edrich rather than with me, to create a different dynamic. It discusses challenges faced and met by Farnell Clarke as the firm has scaled up. Frances talks about standardised workflows, replicable processes and templates to ensure consistent, fair and great quality client service levels across the firm. She cites a time they found four different VAT checklists which resulted in over-servicing clients and undercharging them.

Frances talks about the successes and failures of building an outsource team, as well as the challenges which include recruitment. They discuss the difficulty of moving away from certain roles, and Frances talks about finding someone dedicated to a new service line and the importance of finding people with the right ethos.

Carole asks Frances if she has time to think yet, and they discuss how to make this easier.

Frances talks about the importance of creating a fluid onboarding process for all new clients, and then about how she needs to pass new clients on to the right person or team. She admits that if she didn't keep taking on new projects and tasks that she would have more time to think, and agrees that is unlikely since taking on new projects and tasks is part of her job.

Conversation with Helen Cockle

We talk about the role of AI in the advisory industry. We agree on its great potential and that it has limitations, in particular that it is not a substitute for human insight and judgement.

I note that AI can be useful for tasks such as data analysis and report generation, but that it is not yet capable of providing true and valuable insight. I emphasised that the human element is critical in the creation of client insights, and that AI should be viewed as a tool to augment human expertise rather than a replacement for it.

Helen agrees, and states that the human piece is critical in advisory. She expresses concern that some clients may be overly focused on automation and may request auto-generated Board packs that lack value or insight. She emphasises that not everything should be automated just because it can be, that the human element is necessary to provide true value to clients and explains why Futrli decided to use algorithms rather than AI.

The conversation also includes the importance of trust in the advisory industry, and that while clients are more likely to trust humans than machines, AI could be used to enhance the trust-building process by providing data-driven insights that support human recommendations. Both agree that with or without AI, such an approach could help build trust with clients and enable advisors to provide more personalised and effective recommendations.

We speculate about risks associated with AI in the advisory industry including ethical considerations such as the potential for bias, and the need to ensure that AIs are transparent and accountable. Helen suggests that advisors should be transparent about their use of AI and ensure that clients understand how it is being used. We discuss the impact of blockchain tech on accounting and acknowledge there are still many unknowns.

The conversation concludes with a discussion of the future of AI in the advisory industry. We talk about how the area is changing rapidly and the need for advisors to develop their own skills and expertise in the area of advisory tech, in order to stay ahead of the curve.

Conversation with James Kay

This conversation, which is between James Kay – who I know and work with daily – and Carole Edrich rather than with me, discuss the growth and evolution of Farnell Clarke. James talks about how growth and scaling from three to over 100 people has necessitated a constantly evolving approach. James explains how the struggle to find employees who can think strategically, see the big picture and have the Farnell Clarke vision has been challenging, which has had a knock on effect in terms of building a strong management team and on scaling.

They also discuss the importance of client experience and how Farnell Clarke uses tools like NPS and surveys to gauge how well they meet clients' needs. James emphasises the importance of communication and building strong relationships with clients to retain clients over the long term, and acknowledges the challenges involved in standardising a high quality client experience across different departments.

Carole asks James if Farnell Clarke needs to 'de-James' in a similar way that the firm had to 'de-Will' in the past referring to the need to let go of control and delegate more. James explains that senior team members have come on board to take some of their responsibilities, and that he has carved up his role and delegated as much as he can, but still needs to link everything together and ensure the business is successful.

James also discusses the human side of the firm, emphasising the importance of hiring the right people and building strong teams. He notes that happy teams who work well together have a positive impact on the client experience, and that when they do work well together the client experience is excellent.

Conversation with James Lizars

In a broad ranging conversation we covered topics of ethics, sustainability, purpose, profitability and what James wants to be able to say to his sons. James argued that while companies are made to create profits, most business owners have a broader purpose, and that he wanted to be able to contribute positively by example, to clients and in terms of what he will achieve, whilst also mentioning that being a pauper who has planted a million trees is a bit silly.

James believes that sustainability should be a key aspect of his company and explains his thought processes getting there. While not explicitly his purpose, his work towards moving his firm to net zero shapes the way his business develops in a positive way.

We also discuss how sustainability might stimulate another business line, how smaller businesses are becoming better served by tools that suit them in this area and the broader trend towards purpose-driven business models.

Conversation with John Toon

In a long conversation with John about current and future visions we discuss how accounting might look in five years, ten years and in a hypothetical future.

This includes the medium (5 year) and longer term (10+ year) future of RPA, the pragmatic choices that larger firms must make now and in the future with regards to the balance between on-prem and Cloud-based processes (or their hybridisation), how long such hybrid tech environments might last and the reasons why he believes these things. We then discuss the range of potential opportunities for accountancy firms now and in the longer term future. John talks about how his firm already uses external data feeds to provide additional client insights and speculates how this might change in the future. We end by agreeing that the biggest challenge – to understand how to stay human, use the tech and provide true human-centric insights – will need constant reassessment.

Conversation
with Kenji Kuramoto

We discuss the challenges and trade-offs of selling a business, with a slight diversion on what the future will bring. Kenji talks about how his accounting firm, Acuity has grown from 10 people to 150 over the past decade, but he sometimes misses the simpler times when he knew all of his clients personally. He talks how this is balanced by how he is motivated by the goal of positively impacting more entrepreneurs, and how he recognises the trade-offs that come with scaling, such as not being able to know all his team members.

I mention that Acuity's 25 to 30 per cent revenue growth is impressive, especially when compared to the UK's top accounting firms which average only five per cent. We agree that clarity of purpose is key to driving this growth, and Kenji believes that getting feedback from his team has been most helpful in determining how fast they can grow and scale. He shares a story about how the team cheered when he announced they wouldn't be acquiring another firm that year, and his realisation of just how severely challenging and uncomfortable the rapid inorganic growth from previous acquisitions had been for them.

Kenji explains that his team is the firm's biggest asset, and that the firm pays close attention to their happiness and wellness through monthly surveys. He also shares how he sends out videos to help foster a sense of belonging and culture, and acknowledges that he can't know all of his team members at the level he used to, as the company grows. Despite the challenges, Kenji is committed to scaling Acuity to positively impact more small businesses.

Conversation
with Karen Kennedy

We talk about how Karen's business is focussed on providing accountancy services to local business owners within a 50-mile radius of her rural community in the area around the Isle of Skye in the Scottish Highlands. Her business philosophy is community focussed and she wants to serve the businesses in her area that have been overlooked for grants, support to start up.

She talks about the scheme she set up, and how she believes in living the brand and being open and honest about her work and family life. Karen has young children, and her work needs to accommodate them.

She talks about why she doesn't niche in any particular sector, and about how the community focus and work philosophy make it challenging to find the right staff.

Conversation
with Lauren Sanders

We discuss the importance of focusing on client experience as the key driver of business success. We stress the importance of recruiting to shared values, living those values and aligning all aspects of the company with the vision. We talk about how employee experience and client experience are interlinked and mutually dependent, and that any change the firm makes should be centred on the client.

Lauren talks about the importance of being open, honest and transparent when things go wrong because this helps to create a culture where people aren't afraid to admit mistakes, and share learning. She noted that when a client identified an issue with a zero-hour contract, even though the problem was not caused by Farnell Clarke the firm looked at whether there were any checks that could be put into place to prevent other clients from being impacted in the same way. She stresses the importance of transparency and critical self reflection to improve the client experience.

I mention that while progress may not always be simple, having a clear vision and the belief that the firm can get back on track is fundamental along with the importance of being adaptable. We discuss the importance of living the company's values and rewarding and developing employees who share those values, and that these values are tattooed on the walls so that they are constantly in peoples' minds.

Conversation with Maisie Poskett

We discuss the differences in expectations in the workplace, share some of the results of a survey Maisie conducted for those seeking work or in work as accountants. We discuss whether younger generations prioritise work-life balance, meaningful work and a sense of purpose in their careers and whether older generations tend to prioritise stability, job security and financial compensation.

The conversation shifts to changes in working environments over the years. We discuss how the pandemic has accelerated the trend towards remote work, and how it has transformed the industry. We look at the new challenges involved.

Maisie talks about how training has changed over time, with an increasing focus on accommodating different peoples' career plans, along with the level of interactivity. She mentions the use of virtual reality and gamification within training too. We discuss the focus on practical experience essential in today's job market, where employers often value skills and experience over degrees.

Overall this conversation highlights the importance of understanding the changing expectations and needs of different generations in the workplace, talks about the role of technology and the importance of adapting to new tools as well as the importance of practical, hands-on experience in training.

Conversation with Richard Bertin

Our conversation revolves around the future of the accounting profession and the challenges it is likely to face in the coming years. We talk about its constant evolution, and how the profession is becoming more technologically competent, about how because of this differentiation will not be based on a widget, but the wisdom of the advisor. Richard suggests that passing down nuggets of information to the next generation is key to staying relevant and providing value to clients.

We acknowledge that there are already tech players with the capability to provide bookkeeping and more built into an app, and the challenge for the accounting profession is to continue to provide value in the face of this disruption. Richard talks about his own approach, and his experience in wealth management and how that has informed the way he does business with his clients. He also talks about how younger generations flip jobs and have portfolio lifestyles and how he believes that will change the way that accounting works.

Conversation with Rob Brown

Our conversation centres on the challenge that firms have in terms of differentiating themselves in an increasingly competitive market. We agree that technology has levelled the playing field and it is difficult for firms to stand out based on competitive advantage, market share or qualifications. We agree that therefore the human side of the business represents a source of competitive advantage.

I suggest that firms need to walk the talk when it comes to claims of being proactive, innovative or not. Firms need to demonstrate the value of their differentiation, provide evidence of their points of differentiation, and be held accountable for those claims. Rob talks about how clients and candidates are becoming more discerning, and that video case studies, testimonials and related stories are becoming more important to demonstrate the value of a firms' differentiation.

We agree that evidence of differentiation is crucial to stand out in the market. Rob gives an example of a managing partner of a mid-tier firm with a zero-overtime policy. We both talk about the importance of flexibility, and that it is a significant factor in recruitment culture, and that firms need to offer employees the opportunity to balance work and personal lives. We also discuss how we might create a culture that attracts top talent and loyal clients. We agree that firms that can create a culture of work-life balance and flexibility are likely to attract top talent and loyal clients.

Conversation
with Sam Mitcham

We discuss the importance of balancing technology with humanity in accounting. Sam talks about her experience of building relationships with clients, and how she saw it become increasingly rare in the age of automation and live data.

Sam talks about how she quickly became fascinated with the close relationships that clients had with their partners, even as an apprentice accountant. She was intrigued by the communications aspect of these relationships, where partners not only discussed business matters with clients, but also talked about their personal lives. Determined to be a part of these conversations she kept asking, and eventually her boss let her sit in on them.

She talks about witnessing the shift from human-driven to computer-driven processes in the industry, where even the year-end meetings that used to be more personal had become automated. Clients were leaving firms because they felt like they were just a number, with no human interaction. Sam decided to start her own firm, where she could take things slow and focus on building client relationships.

While Sam uses technology in her practice, she also takes the time to get to know her clients personally. She sees the beauty of cloud technology, but wants to replicate the personal relationships she witnessed as a young apprentice. Her clients appreciate the human touch that she brings to these interactions, and many have come from larger firms where they felt overlooked or ignored.

She sees the accounting industry's evolution as similar to the rise of social media, with both having benefits and downsides. She believes that the human element is crucial in accounting, and is committed to bringing that element back into the industry.

Conversation with Stefan Barrett

We talked about how the Digital Firm made sense to Stefan and what he did as a result, Bee Motion's tech progression from desktop to fully automated end-to-end cloud and pod structure. Stefan talked about how he flexes his charging structure and I compared it to Farnell Clarke's banding.

We also touched on tribalism with app providers, discovered that Stefan comes from commerce and how that shaped his approach, and that developed into how Bee Motion's approach to Advisory is embedded in the VAT return process. Stefan also talked about how he manages scope creep, and what firm personality meant to him.

Glosssary

A

AAP –
App Advisory Plus is a whitelabel service offered to firms that want to select the best of the app ecosystem for their clients.

AAT –
Association of Accounting Technicians

Advisory –
give information and recommend action

Added value service –
in addition to standard service

AI –
artificial intelligence

AML –
Anti Money Laundering

API –
application programming interface

AutoEntry –
automated data entry software

B

Blockchain –
a software platform for digital assets

C

Companies House –
the UK's registrar of companies and an executive agency and trading fund of Her Majesty's Government

CRM –
customer relationship management

CLV –
client lifetime value

Cloud accounting –
using cloud-based services online

CVP –
Client Value Proposition. A statement that defines the unique benefit a product or service provides to its customers.

D

Dext –
automated receipt processing software, formerly ReceiptBank

E

EVP –
Employee Value Proposition is the unique set of benefits and rewards that the firm offers its employees

Expensify –
a software company that provides a travel and expense web and mobile application

Experience Map –
A visual representation of what people/users/clients do, think and feel over time, from the point they start needing a service to when they stop using it

F

FreeAgent –
online accounting software

G

General ledger or GL –
record of total financial accounts

GoCardless –
an online direct debit network that manages a client's recurring payments how and when they want

GoProposal –
pricing and proposal software for accountancy firms

H

HMRC –
UK Tax Authority

I

ICAAP –
Internal Capital Adequacy Assessment Process (ICAAP) Comprises strategies and processes used by banks to assess and maintain, on an ongoing basis, the amounts, types and distribution of internal capital that they consider adequate to cover the nature and level of the risks to which they are or might be exposed

Ignition –
client onboarding assistance software

In-Prem –
in-house/not on the cloud

Intuit –
accounting and tax preparation software for accountants, small businesses and individuals

IPL –
Initial Program Load, a mainframe term for the loading of the operating system into the computer's main memory

K

KashFlow –
online accounting software

KYC –
Know Your Client, an AML acronym

M

MTD –
Making Tax Digital, the UK Governments much delayed initiative for digitalisation of tax

N

NPS or Net Promoter Score –
a system for gauging client satisfaction

O

OCR –
Optical Character Recognition is the electronic or mechanical conversion of images of typed, handwritten or printed text into machine-encoded text

Onboarding –
the orientation process by which a new client or employee learns the ropes and culture of a new company

Outprice –
to sell at a lower price than another company/seller

P

Porters Strategies –
four generic categories by which you can attain competitive advantage

Product Parity –
similarities between products that make them substitutable

Q

QuickBooks –
an accounting software package

R

ReceiptBank –
automated receipt processing software, now Dext

ROI –
return on investment

ROO –
return on objective

RTI –
Real Time Information

S

Sage50 –
desktop accounting software

Sage Business Cloud Accounting –
cloud-based accounting software for small and medium-sized businesses

Son of MTD –
Shorthand for HMRC's reinvention of Making Tax Digital

Super-evolution –
the fast and seamless scaled growth of an organisation through consistent change based on fulfilling the organisation's purpose

T

Tech stack –
all the tech and apps a company uses

Touchpoint –
any time a potential or current customer comes in contact with you or your brand, before, during or after they are your client

V

VUCA –
Volatility, Uncertainty, Complexity and Ambiguity, describing a business environment characterised by rapid and unpredictable changes, high levels of uncertainty, intricate interdependencies and vague or incomplete information

W

Wfh –
abbreviation for Working From Home

X

Xero –
cloud-based accounting software for small and medium-sized businesses

Printed in Great Britain
by Amazon